Therese Quinn & Erica R. Meiners

FLAUNT IT!
Queers Organizing for Public Education and Justice

PETER LANG
New York • Washington, D.C./Baltimore • Bern
Frankfurt am Main • Berlin • Brussels • Vienna • Oxford

Library of Congress Cataloging-in-Publication Data
Quinn, Therese.
Flaunt it!: queers organizing for public education and justice /
Therese Quinn, Erica R. Meiners.
p. cm. — (Counterpoints: studies in the postmodern theory of education; v. 340)
Includes bibliographical references and index.
1. Privatization in education—Social aspects—United States.
2. Homosexuality and education—United States. I. Meiners, Erica R. II. Title.
LB2806.36.Q85 370.86'64—dc22 2008054708
ISBN 978-1-4331-0265-3
ISSN 1058-1634

Bibliographic information published by **Die Deutsche Bibliothek**.
Die Deutsche Bibliothek lists this publication in the "Deutsche
Nationalbibliografie"; detailed bibliographic data is available
on the Internet at http://dnb.ddb.de/.

Cover art by Damon Locks

The paper in this book meets the guidelines for permanence and durability
of the Committee on Production Guidelines for Book Longevity
of the Council of Library Resources.

Printed in the United States of America

FLAUNT IT!

Studies in the
Postmodern Theory of Education

Joe L. Kincheloe and Shirley R. Steinberg
General Editors

Vol. 340

PETER LANG
New York • Washington, D.C./Baltimore • Bern
Frankfurt am Main • Berlin • Brussels • Vienna • Oxford

For Octavia Butler (1947 – 2006)
and Harriet McBryde Johnson (1957 – 2008)
who taught the pleasures of imagining and resistance.

CONTENTS

Foreword
    by Catherine Lugg   ix

Introduction   Queers in Public and Other Riots   1

Chapter 1   Straightening Unruly Bodies through Military Education   13

Chapter 2   "Lightning Rods": Public Educational Policies,
the *Shadow State,* and the Queer   29

Chapter 3   Redlining for the Lavender Menace:
Covenants, Privatopias, and Restricting Undesirables   43

Chapter 4   Troubled Gender:
Nations, Teaching Professions, and Covering   61

Chapter 5   Studying Up: Policy Activism   75

Conclusion   Volatile Affect:
Resisting Shame and Stigma in the Profession   95

Afterword
    by Lisa Yun Lee   105

References   109

Index   127

FOREWORD

Historically, education has been part of the "helping professions." As in the fields of nursing and social work, most aspirants become public school teachers for both vocational and advocational reasons. We like working with children and young adults, and we want to make a difference in our students' lives, as well as to build a better community. Given the ongoing poor working conditions of most public schools and the vast funding and resource inequities across schools that are supposedly "common" to all children, those public school teachers who remain in the profession do so for largely intrinsic—not extrinsic—reasons. And some of these intrinsic reasons include working for greater human and civil rights for all children.

With the professionalization of educational research and the subsequent rise of major educational research associations, this tradition of educator advocacy has become an increasingly "inconvenient truth." Educators who move into the research arena can be scolded by our peers for being "too political" and "not objective" when we ground our scholarly work in our social justice commitments—commitments that were held long before our doctoral degrees. In the United States, where public education has been distributed along lines of race, ethnicity, class, sex, gender, religion, language, sexual orientation, and dis/ability, social justice–oriented educational scholarship can be labeled as "emotional," "political," "subjective," or even "me-search" (instead of "re-search"). This kind of labeling is a political tactic, an attempt to get these unruly scholars to "shut up" and/or "go away." Social justice–oriented scholars ask uncomfortable and disturbing questions, questions that can be downright impolite and even impertinent in elite circles. Power and the powerful are being held accountable—whether they like it or not.

In *Flaunt It!*, Therese Quinn and Erica Meiners draw on their well-grounded commitments to queer and social justice activism to ask some uncomfortable research questions. These questions involve the privatization and militarization of urban public schools (while the public retains control in the affluent and largely white suburbs), the influence of anti-queer organizations upon private educational agencies in shaping "accreditation standards" for educator preparation programs, the studied silence of the world's largest educational research organization on most issues of social justice while concurrently mealy-mouthing social justice nostrums, and the myriad problems of having only "nice white ladies" teach in U.S. public schools. Quinn and Meiners pose these questions in a forthright manner, not softened by the academiceeze that pervades much educational scholarship. Additionally, Quinn and Meiners' explorations of these questions combine a healthy dose of queer attitude and unflinching analyses. Quite simply, *flaunting it* becomes an interrogative, an analysis, and a form of educator action.

As you read *Flaunt It!*, I invite the reader to sit down, settle in, and remember *why* you became an educator. But don't just sit there after reading this book. You are a moral and political agent living and working in a supposedly democratic republic. You have a voice and I suggest that you flaunt it.

Catherine Lugg, Rutgers University

INTRODUCTION
Queers in Public and Other Riots

In response to public scenes of joy and love in San Francisco in 2004, Governor Arnold Schwarzenegger stated on NBC's *Meet the Press* that he wanted a halt to the runaway same-sex marriages because he feared widespread chaos, even revolution:

> All of a sudden, we see riots, we see protests, we see people clashing. The next thing we know, there is injured or there is dead people. We don't want it to get to that extent...We cannot have mayors all of a sudden go hand out licenses for various things. In the next city, it'll be handing out licenses for assault weapons. In the next, it'll be someone handing them out to sell drugs. (Schwarzenegger as quoted in Epstein, 2004, ¶3, ¶14)

The Governator saw bedlam in the streets. What we saw was elation: long queues of crazily happy women and men outside City Hall, lined up to register and celebrate their unions with flowers, music, snacks, and fabulous outfits. Sure, we could also say it looked like another triumph of capitalism, and local governments are indeed fully aware of the financial impact of marrying couples—a 2008 study commissioned by Massachusetts, for example, estimated that allowing out-of-state lesbian and gay couples to marry there would generate 330 permanent jobs and add $111 million to the economy over three years (Belluck & Zezima, 2008). As feminists and queers—the latter a term we use in two ways throughout this book: first, as we do here, to encompass not just gay, lesbian, bisexual, and transgendered identities but all non-heteronormative and non-gender–conforming identifications (de Lauretis, 1991); and next, from queer theory, as a way to push back at normalized social conceptions in the broadest sense (Warner, 1999)—we are no fans of "legal" marriage for anyone. Instead, like earlier women's and gay liberationists, we imagine how we can all become more "free to shape creative and pleasurable relations with other human beings" (McRuer, 2008, ¶3). Still, we are fully aware of the more than 1,049 federal and additional state protections, benefits, and responsibilities attached to marriage, according to the federal government's General Accounting Office (Duggan, 2004). Love is always worth a celebration, but *access*—to health care, immigration, housing, bereavement benefits, and the other life-shaping tangibles that should be "human- not marriage-rights" (McRuer, 2008, ¶6)—was the powerful undercurrent to the day's events and emotions. In this context, Schwarzenegger's fearful and fear-mongering statements identify the power of the queer body and its potential to call into question fragile demarcations: public/private, normal/abnormal, and sanctioned/outlawed (Warner, 1999).

We—two queer teacher educators in Chicago—work on a wide range of justice issues, including prison abolition, educational equity, affordable housing, and more. For us, queerness is radical when it fosters, as Mattilda Bernstein Sycamore (2006) contends, an "outsider perspective" that calls us to "challenge everything that's sickening about the dominant cultures" (p. 8). This book chronicles our response to that call—in these pages, we tell the story of our queer resistance to the implementation of Department of Defense-run schools in the Chicago Public Schools system; our work organizing against the largest national teacher-education accreditation agency's removal of sexual orientation and social justice from its accreditation standards; our protests of our state's decision to hold a public meeting for teacher educators at a private Christian college that condemns homosexuality; and our collaborative policy activism to audit LGBTQ visibility in teacher preparation programs across the state of Illinois. While theorizing our participation in these schooling sites, an interesting contraction emerged: Public education is being reformed through appeals to "private choice," and at the same time select public issues, especially those that address the invisibility and rejection of queers and our lives within education, are devalued by being called private.

Spectacularly public queer bodies incite riots and may do violence to the state, Schwarzenegger seems to claim, by opening up too many possibilities, and so containment by any and every means is essential. Yet, strategies to control and corral induce contradictions. Anti–gay marriage amendments and measures crop up during election year like crabgrass, while "domestic partnership" benefits are increasingly de rigueur in most for-profit, private Fortune 500 companies (Holt, 2004; Gunther, 2006). In May 2008, the California Supreme Court narrowly endorsed gay and lesbian marriages (subsequently overturned by the Proposition 8 referendum), yet in 2008 the Michigan Supreme Court slammed the door on domestic partner benefits (Liptak, 2008; Jaschik, 2008). Presidential candidates in the 2008 election tripped over themselves to demonstrate their support of traditional—one man and one woman— marriages, yet Republican candidate John McCain appeared on the TV show *Ellen* touting his "respect for their differences" and its out lesbian host Ellen DeGeneres asked McCain to walk her down the aisle ("DeGeneres needles McCain," 2008). Some states and municipalities offer domestic partner benefits and protection from discrimination in employment and housing, while other states and municipalities have passed "reverse" discrimination statutes and laws highlighting that gays and lesbians do not have equal rights.

Historically, courts have only added to this confusion. Not unlike the variances in the United States when the courts routinely shifted gears on "who got to be white" and, therefore, could benefit from the social, economic, and political privileges affiliated with whiteness, (López, 1996; Harris, 1993; Roediger, 1991), the lack of clarity surrounding public protections for sexual orientation is as muddled as the shifting official terminology: moral degeneracy, perversion, homosexuality, sexual preference, alternative lifestyle, lifestyle choices, sexual orientation, and more. In particular, without the protections of direct public policies or constitutional rights from the courts, or without being afforded the privacy to be simply ignored, the queer body continues to inflame the nation's anxieties.

Specifically, it is the queer teacher that incites the most rage and mobilizations against sexual minorities. From the failed 1978 Briggs Measure in California that aimed to bar all out, not closeted, homosexuals from teaching, to the 1992 Oregon ballot measure stating, "All governments in Oregon may not use their monies or properties to promote, encourage or facilitate homosexuality, pedophilia, sadism or masochism. All levels of government, including public education systems, must assist in setting a standard for Oregon's youth which recognizes that these behaviors are abnormal, wrong, unnatural and perverse and they are to be discouraged and avoided" (Anderson, 2006, p. 148), schools are deeply, compulsively, heteronormative spaces. Again in 2000, a reworded Measure 9 was introduced in Oregon, seeking to prohibit school employees from "encouraging, promoting, sanctioning homosexual, bisexual behaviors" among students; it, too, was narrowly defeated ("Anti-Gay Measure," 2000).

Across the United States, teachers are expected to support the social-reproduction purposes of schools and are assumed to be heterosexual and "models of...values" (Khayatt, 1992, p. 146). However, by definition, queer teachers disrupt the assumption of values congruence when they are known or out in their schools. But even when unknown and unlabeled, queers can trigger "moral" or "sex panic" in schools (Rofes, 2005, p. 94). Heteronormativity, the structures and systems "that legitimize and privilege heterosexuality and heterosexual relationships as fundamental and 'natural' within society" (Cohen, 2005, p. 24), is pervasive in most institutions, including schools. Fear of the "queer," or all the meanings and associations attached to non-heteronormativity, can lead schools to suppress teachers and teachers to censor students (and themselves)—the kind of fear that in 2008 caused one student even to kill a same-sex Valentine-giving peer (Russell, 2008). In this context, remembering and reclaiming the "radical potential of queer identity" is more important than ever and is the impulse that inspired this book (Sycamore, 2006, p. 8).

The book is divided into chapters, each composed of a description of the local contexts for our work and our questions, a sociopolitical analysis, and, where relevant, documents that we have produced. Using our work organizing against the military's incursions into the public schools, Chapter One discusses the privatization of the public sphere. Chapter Two focuses on the de facto erasure of sexual orientation and the active removal of social justice from the primary U.S. teacher accreditation organization. Beginning with the story of our trip to a private Christian college with an anti-gay "covenant," Chapter Three illustrates the role of the profession in supporting a culture of silence and silencing in public education when the bodies and the issues are queer and includes an analysis of historic and contemporary systems of exclusion. Chapter Four explores professionalism: we start with a look at the history of gender and whiteness in teaching and investigate how this context has shaped organizing. Chapter Five offers an example of collective policy activism; it documents our work on a statewide electronic audit of the visibility of LGBTQ lives and rights in Illinois's colleges and universities, especially within their teacher education programs. We close with feelings. While emotions are woven throughout these narratives, our Conclusion addresses how some—in particular, anger and shame—are used to regulate the borders between the public and the private and work to silence queers. This discussion frames feelings as public and political, central to activism, and an important component of participatory research. We finish with the start of a manifesto, a desire for a do-it-yourself kit, and reflections on the strategies that we explicate in the book. We invite you to add, challenge, reframe, and adapt.

At the risk of marking ourselves and our projects "unprofessional," we insist that a commentary on our process and the economies within which this work will circulate is pivotal, and offer next a brief overview of the themes, questions, methods, feelings, and observations that emerged while doing this work and writing this book.

The Shifting Terrain of Public and Private

Concepts of identity and choice are intertwined and are integral to the particular erosions of public education in the United States. Framing issues as private is a political act that, ironically, aims to remove certain identities, including women, people of color, and the disabled—and the bodies and labor attached to them—from economic and political contexts. For example, childcare is considered a private issue, as are maternity benefits, *domestic* violence, and in-home personal assistance for disabled people. Classification as private absolves the community and government from assuming responsibility. This trick is more than rhetorical and not confined to the contemporary political scene. For

example, "personal responsibility" has been offered by everyone from Booker
T. Washington to Bill Clinton as the answer to problems—from poverty to
illness—experienced by low-income Americans of color. Yet, while particular
lives and experiences are erased as private, other issues are labeled public but
are nevertheless tied to sensibilities and discourses—the free market, in particular—that actively mask social effects and culpabilities. Who hasn't heard,
as public housing is torn down to make way for pricey condominiums, foreclo-
sures mount, and affordable rents disappear, that no one is responsible for this
massive displacement of peoples and communities? It's just "the market."

Reframing the public sphere through *personal responsibility* and an imagined *private* world is a hallmark of contemporary neoliberalism—a framework
aimed at opening up all parts of society to the free market, which is notable for
qualities such as "competition, inequality, market 'discipline,' public austerity,
and 'law and order'" (Duggan, 2003, p. x). Worldwide, neoliberalism signifies
economic, political, and social shifts that promote deregulation and privatization, and the rise of a supposedly unencumbered and unassisted marketplace.
In the United States, the neoliberal remaking of institutions and practices,
from utility services to schools, continues to be forged not through coups or
military might, but, as David Harvey (2005) states, through the "long march"
of corporations, media, think-tanks, and other powerful private for-profit
forces that have sought to change not only economic and political policies but
also the cultural understandings that ground our relationship to democracy
(Harvey, p. 40). This has particular ramifications for those already located on
the margins of the social, economic, and political mainstream. Indeed, privatization in public economic and political spheres—whether of charter schools
that prohibit teacher union memberships, or never-ending wars fought by con-
tracted security forces, or mass incarcerations and the growth industry of private prisons—requires parallel privatizing transformations in how we
understand our identities, families, emotions, and relations to the state. For
example, queer issues are produced to be "too confrontational and threatening
as public debate and too ridiculous, trivial and inappropriate *for* public institutions" (Duggan, 2003, p. 40). Acts such as touching and kissing, when enacted
by queers in public spaces are construed as spectacularly, wildly disruptive.
What about raising queer issues as they relate to schools? Extremely trouble-
some—"flaunting it," as one of us was told by her associate dean. Queers are
clearly present in "public" realms (schools, for example), yet all of our lives
and concerns are framed as private, ours alone, and not of broader social im-
port. For queers, then, *public* and *private* form a binary through which oppression is reinforced.

Throughout this book we use a queer lens to explore policies and practices
that shape the lives of youth, communities, and teachers in our schools. Posing

challenges to our nation's reliance on borders and incarceration, the militarization of everyday life, and the privatization of services essential for the "common good," this book addresses issues vital to the lives of many, including
queers. For us, queer organizing means, as Sycamore writes, "fighting racism,
fighting classism, fighting homophobia: you can't take them apart" (in Sycamore, with Ruiz, 2008, p. 238). But, while we urge the queering of social—
always including racial and economic—justice, we argue that it is as imperative
that sexual and gender politics are named within sites of struggle that have
often passed as "gender neutral" or "queer free." Simultaneously, we must
challenge what the state, or community, frames as a "gay issue."

"Gay marriage" is a topical example of the importance of challenging what
are presented as gay and lesbian issues in the United States. Marriage—as of
2008, legal for gay men and lesbians in two U.S. states—brings with it a host
of benefits for same-sex couples who choose to marry. But, this access is offered at a moment when fewer individuals receive *any* state support or protection. Readers, we are certain, can name a myriad ways that employment and
political rights have been whittled away in recent decades; other social needs
have never been addressed. We'll offer a few we have noted: The decimation
of unions and the concurrent explosion of contingent and "just in time" workers without benefits; the eradication of public housing and the challenges to
rent control; the continued denial of childcare or maternity benefits; the fifty
million Americans without health insurance; the shift from welfare to workfare. And, let us not forget: the United States is disenfranchisement central.
According to a 2007 report from the Sentencing Project, "5.3 million Americans, or one in forty-one adults, have currently or permanently lost their voting rights as a result of a felony conviction" (Sentencing Project, 2007, p. 1). In
addition to those housed in prison, or those with voting prohibitions linked to
convictions, the Pew Hispanic Trust estimates that approximately twelve to
fifteen million residents across the United States are undocumented and are
thus denied access to the vote despite the reality that many of these residents
are workers and pay taxes (Pew Hispanic Trust, 2006). These are just some of
the most visible markers of our crumbling public sphere and the impact of
neoliberal policies.

At the same time, it seems to us that gay marriage debases the most radical
promises of queerness—that all our loves matter; that families are made
through love, not given by law; that passion itself is fruitful—and concedes too
easily: we will be just like everyone else, wholesome, the marrying kinds, if you
stop calling us perverts and give us a few "rights." Thus, we suggest paying
careful attention to *feelings* in these private and public proposals. In the current
gay marriage debate, lesbians and gays are being asked to make a deal: our

queer solidarity with all the other "others" without rights, in exchange for good feelings, tax exemptions, and toasters. This rough trade—not the pleasurable kind—reminds us to follow the feelings and affect in our own and others' work because emotions shape political and economic mobilizations. Shame, fear, disgust, and loneliness, these and other social motivators push queers toward the "new homonormativity… a politics that does not contest dominant heteronormative assumptions and institutions, but upholds and sustains them, while promising the possibility of a…privatized, depoliticized gay culture anchored in domesticity and consumption" (Duggan, 2003, p. 50).

The 2007 Employment Non-Discrimination Act (ENDA) debates are another clear example of homonormative strategies in practice and forms a useful counterpoint to the gay marriage example. When ENDA moved into the all-Democratic House in 2006, the bill included sexual orientation and gender identity and expression. This was endorsed by almost all mainstream gay and lesbian organizations. Yet, the bill's sponsor, Barney Frank, decided to strip gender identity from the bill in order to ensure that it would pass and placed gender identity in a separate bill. The bill supporting protection from employment discrimination for gays and lesbians (sexual orientation) passed, but not the one that included gender identity (Stryker, 2008, pp. 150–151). Heteronormativity and homophobia are weapons of sexism—the fear of being called queer supports normative gender performances. Similarly, transphobia operates within the logic of sexism by regulating gender roles. The ENDA bill prohibits discrimination on the basis of sexual orientation but does not protect gender non-conformity. Not only is discrimination against transmen and transwomen in employment and other areas severe, the failure to include gender identity *actively harms* lesbians and gays, and arguably, everyone.

> Most discrimination against gay, lesbian and bisexual people who were not transgendered was rooted in prejudice about gender normative appearances and behaviors—that is, it was the too effeminate gay man, or the too masculine woman, who was more vulnerable to employment discrimination than straight looking, straight acting, homosexual men and women. (Stryker, 2008, p. 151)

Just as the promise of gay marriage offers little to few and denies much to many, the ENDA example also illustrates another facet of public "queer" policy initiatives. Strategies that turn on assimilative politics or that deny the fullness of queer expression and lives do little to make our communities—all of them—more just.

The price of assimilation for "good gays" in this political landscape is the willingness to close our eyes to the millions, and rising, locked out of any access to rights, including the "bad gays" who are criminalized (Warner, 1999). Gay marriage, in other words, is the promise of membership in a club with less and less to offer. And, notably, these shifting constructions of access to rights and de facto to full citizenship are also shaped by, and through, *feelings*. It feels good to have one's worth validated through inclusion, and not so good to be singled out as the kind of different that equals bad or wrong. In this book, we struggle through questions central to queer and justice organizing across the United States.

> What kind of sexual rights should we be fighting for? Is the goal a more inclusive private life or a public sexual culture that might be shared by all? If we contest the privatization at the heart of American neoliberalism, the ways in which the public is increasingly policed and controlled by corporations, we must also recognize that our claims to citizenship are grounded in this shrinking private sphere. (Weiss, 2008, pp. 97–98)

These issues must be debated in public and with as many participants as possible. *Deviant, ex-con, alien, welfare queen, pervert*—the queer body, produced as spectacular, incites *outlaw* relationalities. However, we suggest that, rather than negating these connections, we work in solidarity with these linkages—we are all in it together.

An Archive of Labor, Pleasure, and Participatory Research

This book documents our *participatory research* (PR)—a methodology with connections to social justice movements and popular education through which "ordinary" people aim to understand what affects their lives (Park, 2001, p. 83; Lewis, 2006)—on the effects of privatized public education on queers. Participatory research (PR) centers on individuals making changes to "improv[e] the material circumstances" of their lives (Park, 2001, p. 83); they do this by identifying issues, gathering data, engaging in reflection and analysis, and taking action. Participatory research is improvisational and often conducted by people who are not authorized by their credentials or expertise to "be" researchers. We distinguish PR from participatory action research (PAR) because through the projects chronicled in this book, our primary aim is not to describe our work partnering as academics and researchers *with* youth, or *with* other marginalized communities, to support *their* actions for social change (Borda, 2001; Heron & Reason, 2001). We do, in many of the projects outlined in this book, work alongside youth, parents, and others struggling for equity and access to resources and justice. However, the projects outlined in this book identify primarily our attempts to engage ourselves in new ways as activists *within our profession*. As social geographers Linda Peake and Audrey Kobayashi (2002) note, "participation...is a fundamental method of antiracist [and all social justice] research" (p. 55). Through the model of PR, which prioritizes linking our professional work to our quotidian selves, we hope to encourage other scholars to act without waiting for "expertise" or institutional permission.

Further, because this project is about the discursive and material strategies that are used by the state and the right to make some individuals' acts and lives invisible, this book works to interrupt erasure by presenting artifacts from our daily work and organizing efforts.

> An archive is not simply a repository; it is also a theory of cultural relevance, a construction of collective memory, and a complex record of queer activity. (Halberstam 2005, p. 170)

Specifically, we contribute to the project of archiving the evidence of queer existence by including, in full and part, original texts—letters, flyers, emails, petitions, and pledges—that document conflicts involving queerness.

Archiving is a vital component of participatory research. In crafting responses to the situations recorded in this book, we devised tactics on the fly, looking for opportunities of the moment; this, de Certeau (1984) suggests, is the defining characteristic of a tactic—it "makes use of the cracks" (p. 37). But these emergent and opportunistic ploys are evanescent, while the need for justice-work is ongoing and dependent on a populace coming together to initiate change. Thus, *sharing* our tactics of resistance seems vital; it charts a course that someone once followed and could be followed again, encouraging participation. At the same time, we hope this archive invites innovation: as the hackers' maxim goes, "Information wants to be free." Finally, using the tactic of pushing back against the privatizing of feelings by framing them as information *in* and *for* a public may also help to create the coalescing space that social movements need. Public movements, as long-time activist Bernardine Dohrn states, are the "oxygen of a participatory democracy" (Dorhn, 2008).

In addition to archiving and generating knowledge from participatory research, this volume uses multiple frameworks and knowledge bases. This is a transdisciplinary project (Nader, 2005): it recognizes that the question of justice in schools and society cannot be addressed simply through one theoretical lens, and that queer struggles can never be defined in isolation from struggles for justice and equity *by, for,* and *with* other communities. For example, when state resources for prison expansion and policing balloon, fewer dollars are available for youth employment programs, and for schools, community colleges, and universities. Educational issues are always about society's normative pressures, thus, they are always about queer, disability, racial, and gender rights. And, sustaining a high-quality public education system requires that communities must also provide affordable housing and healthcare; therefore, public education is always enmeshed with other public policies. In other words, this book, detailing as it does our work for justice in public education,

could not be neatly limited to one discipline, canon, methodology, or movement. We have benefited from the insights offered by many authors who are
positioned both inside and outside a range of movements and fields, and our
work here reflects their insights, as we've noted throughout our writing. These
influential authors include queer theorists who discuss the importance of feelings for political movement building, social and economic geographers who
examine the decline of public space, a critical race theorist's construct of "covering," feminist activists and scholars, organizers and teachers who work on
policy and queer educational issues, and many others.

This archive also documents projects initiated and sustained without outside funding. We are not martyrs—we did consider hustling some cash but
simply never got around to it. But for us, the bottom line was doing the work,
with or without a budget. In any case, as the organization INCITE! Women of
Color Against Violence has suggested—the revolution will not be funded
(INCITE, 2007). We note this to encourage you: Don't wait for a recipe, a
grant, institutional approval, or optimum conditions to do the good hard work
that needs to be done—just get started. To paraphrase Marc Bousquet's invitation to activism in academia, we can't promise you a revolution (as much as
we'd like to be able to), but we *can* guarantee you the pleasure of some very
butch and femme shoulders to lean on as we toil at these tasks together.[1]

Naming the absence of capital in the form of funds, time, and other resources is important now as there is an increasing emphasis at public and private academic institutions on acquiring external funding, and this push shapes
the research professors develop: Universities are not neutral sites in the decline
of the industrial empire. As Bousquet notes in his account of postsecondary
corporations as industries of labor exploitation, "Late capitalism doesn't just
happen to the university; *the university makes late capitalism happen*"
(Bousquet, 2008, p. 44, emphasis original). With the failure of the tenured
professoriate to stem the explosion of part-time knowledge workers, prohibi-
tive tuition costs at public and private postsecondary institutions, and the exploitation of student labor under the guise of learning, universities and faculty
are not outside of or exempt from the effects of neoliberalism. As institutions
that reproduce social and economic classes and legitimize what counts as
knowledge and who counts as knowledge makers, schools of higher education
are at the heart of the matter; professors are *embedded* in the rusting machinery
of these systems. We must question our roles in the exploitation of others and
then match words to work. To that end, we offer this book.

---

[1] From his foreword to *Workplace: A Journal for Academic Labor.*

Yet, throughout this book, we use the expressions *activism* and *organizing* somewhat interchangeably, albeit with reservations. As academics, now both tenured, we have twelve-month salaries and a social safety net: retirement benefits, health and dental care, vacation time, control over our working day, and more. In fact, parts of this book were completed over the summer, when neither of us really had to show up at our offices—and we still got paid. And, when we gave a talk about portions of this work at a conference, an audience member scoffed that what we do—"letter writing and all that"—does not count as organizing. We wonder: Are we activists, or are we simply doing what we should be doing as professors of education: writing, participating in civic debate, and paying attention to the crucial issues of the moment? Yet, what does it mean to not use the term *activist*, in this moment when it has acquired such a negative spin in "professional" and political realms? Judges who do not adhere to regressively peculiar "strict" interpretations of the Constitution are, suddenly, *activist judges* who should not hold office (Marcus, 2005). Teachers who include Malcolm X in their curriculum or are queer and out are *activist teachers* (Blume, 2008). And so on. If being activist means working for justice, we are activists, and specifically *activist academics*.

But, we are also aware of ways activism has been misrepresented and romanticized in academia and in activists' ideas and products claimed by researchers in these institutions. As Sycamore (2008) writes, "trickle down academia" is "the process by which academics appropriate anything they can get their hands on and then claim to have invented it" (p. 244). Through our positions in universities, we are irrevocably linked to the system Sycamore describes; but our desire to challenge such colonizing and privatizing practices of knowledge construction also shapes how we have written this book.

Rejecting the traditional academic tics of *disembodied narrator, neutrality,* and claims of *expert knowledge* and *original contribution*, we offer instead narrative descriptions (jointly created), revealed emotions, and many questions. In other words, with this book, we have tried to align our commitments: the projects chronicled and the chronicle itself are fully collaborative productions. We attach this statement to the writing we do together (including this book):

> *This is a co-authored work with equal contributions from each of us and no first author. The order in which we are listed is based on a rotation we use in our collaborations on publications.*

We highly recommend this kind of fun partnering to others: it feels good to cut loose from the pressure of "first voice" and "brilliant insight" and acknowledge in this material way that writing is always in some part collective. Offering first-person narratives, revealed emotions, and unanswered questions in jointly claimed writing is a means to resist privatization, our goal throughout the projects discussed here. Our collaboration acknowledges that ideas are public, produced in relationships, through and because of work, and that this materiality is erased by myths of solo originality.

In this book, we work to demonstrate not only that the messy work of participation is what is needed now in education, but also that chronicling this public work and the feelings that fuel and can guide it is research. Far from confessional tales or vanity ethnography (van Maanen, 1988), this book is grounded in praxis: archiving emotions, tactics attempted in public, and reflections on our justice-seeking mobilizations. We invite you to try other tactics that seize on the "crosscuts, fragments, cracks and lucky hits in the framework of a system" (de Certeau, 1984, p. 38) and ask that you, too, archive and distribute this work, as we have done here, to expose the fissures in power that make institutions vulnerable and build communities of resistance along the way to change.

The stories we tell in the chapters that follow are not redemptive: We can't delight you with tales of the hero-academic who sweeps in to save the day with brilliance and a new vocabulary for old problems, or the missionary who finds humanity and some cool new style while doing time with the natives, or the activist-expert who is too busy to attend a meeting but has plenty of stories about days spent on the frontline. Rather, our accounts are of struggles. We tell these with some confidence, not because we are experts, but because we have done the work outlined in this book. We have also made mistakes and keep learning. Most of all, we continue to act.

CHAPTER 1

Straightening Unruly Bodies through Military Education

Teachers Against Militarized Education (TAME) Logo.
Artwork by Eric Triantafillou

In 2005, word circulated through our neighborhood (we live a block from each other) that one wing of the local public high school—Nicholas Senn High School—was going to be turned into a naval academy. Senn opened in 1913 in a grand L-shaped building facing a large grassy yard; today this green space is often filled with students drifting away from the building at the close of the day, older neighbors sitting on benches under crabapple trees, and dogs chasing balls. Senn has a largely working-class and immigrant student population, but the neighborhood has been slowly changing, "gentrifying," for years. Some community members, seeking a more rapid increase in property values, expressed concerns that the school's quality and reputation would discourage wealthier residents from relocating to the area. The city's mayor had recently initiated a school reform plan focused on the development of a "choice" system, with each school targeting a different consumer niche. Seizing the moment, the area's alderwoman, Mary Ann Smith, OK'd an arrangement in which the local navy base gave the fledgling military school a start-up fund, and she gave the school one wing of Senn's building. The last to be notified about these agreements were the teachers, the students, the school administration, and the community, and by that time the plan was being described as a "done deal." After participating in many local meetings as citizens and neighbors, we wondered—as both of us are also professors of education—where were our academic colleagues on this issue? We considered how we might be able to leverage our collective "expertise" to participate in the public policy decisions that were being implemented without input or accountability. Our professor-friends might not all turn out for local community meetings or to protests, but we thought they would endorse a letter that named the ways this process was flawed.

February 4, 2005

Dear Arne Duncan, Mayor Daley, and Members of the Chicago Board of Education:

On December 15, 2004, Chicago's Board of Education voted to approve the establishment of a "Naval Academy" in Senn High School located in Chicago's Edgewater community. One of Chicago's most diverse schools, Senn is home to 1,700 students from more than 65 countries. Good things have been happening at this neighborhood institution—Senn has a successful International Baccalaureate Diploma Program, was recently awarded a five-year $1.2 million grant from the Lloyd A. Fry Foundation to provide development and support services to freshmen and sophomores, and was selected as one of only 16 National Service-Learning Leader Schools.

Despite these and other successes, against the wishes of many Senn teachers, students, and parents, and without a process for community consultation, you decided to install a Naval Academy in Senn High School in fall 2005.

There are many reasons to oppose this decision. The lack of neighborhood involvement is one: It is simply wrong to remake this school without considering community voices and vision. The apparent hypocrisy of city leaders is another: How can the city endorse the military for Chicago Public School students when the Chicago City Council has declared the city a Nuclear Weapon Free Zone and voted to reject the invasion of Iraq and the U.S. Patriot Act? And, as educators, we oppose the proposed Naval Academy, because it and other military academies offer:

Bad education
The evidence is overwhelming that urban military-themed schools fail to provide a high quality education that prepares youth to graduate high school and enter college. Instead of receiving a well-rounded education, students study subjects like "Military Science" and "Army Customs and Courtesies." With that kind of preparation, is it a surprise that at Chicago's Carver Military Academy, similar in

structure to the proposed Naval Academy, only 54% of students graduate from high school, and only 34% of graduating seniors enter college?

Racial targeting
The pattern is clear: The Chicago Board of Education targets low-income, primarily African American, communities for military-themed high schools. Schools for the elite, such as Northside College Prep, are not forced to house military programs. Instead, these schools and their upper-income white communities are offered gifted, magnet, and college prep schools and programs. Imposing a Naval Academy at Senn will reinforce this negative and unfortunately familiar message: *poor youth of color merit substandard education.*

Sanctioned discrimination
"Don't ask, don't tell" is not acceptable for Chicago's gay, lesbian, bisexual and transgendered youth. Although the Chicago Board of Education, City of Chicago, Cook County, and the State of Illinois all prohibit discrimination based on sexual orientation, the United States Military condones discrimination against sexual minorities. Military schools are partnerships between the United States Armed Services and Chicago Public Schools; like San Francisco and Portland, Oregon, Chicago should refuse to allow the military to recruit in its public schools, and refuse to do business with organizations that discriminate against its citizens.

Chicago must provide high quality education equally to all its youth and communities. The racially targeted establishment of military-themed schools is wrong in every case. But in a time of seemingly boundless budgets for endless war it is especially fraught to tell poor kids, "The best education we can offer you is one linked to combat." This is not a "choice," as Arne Duncan has referred to the proposed Naval Academy, it is a tragedy.

As faculty in colleges and programs of education across Chicago, we know this city can do better. And it must.

Sincerely,
53 Concerned Educators

We collected signatures and sent the letter out. The response was near-silence—just one phone call from a local reporter who first asked us which of the letter's signatories were tenured professors and then wrote a short article noting only the letter's existence. There was no reaction from Chicago Public Schools (CPS). The Rickover Naval Academy was dedicated in November 2005 and opened in fall 2006. CPS then announced a plan to establish military themed, funded, and operated schools throughout Chicago (Anchors Away, 2007). We geared up to distribute the letter again.

According to CPS, parental preference is driving the expansion of the military schools. But Senn insiders claim there is no great demand for places in the Naval Academy. The school "did not meet their quota of 125 [admitted students] by the middle of [the summer before opening]" (Save Senn, 2006). And, in fact, Rickover is still under-enrolled today, in 2008.

The issue of queer youth was raised in our letter and yet remained unaddressed in community organizing against militarized schools (although we attended many meetings and events on the issue, we heard only one other individual raise LGBTQ issues in connection to the militarization of schools). Later, after we sent her a copy of the letter, Alderwoman Toni Preckwinkle, a local politician working toward a moratorium on the establishment of military schools, bluntly stated, "If anti-war sentiments can't sell this [moratorium], the gay issue certainly won't do it. It's a non-starter." Within the neighborhood, we kept organizing, attending public meetings, and participating in rallies and events designed to keep some media attention on the issue of militarizing schools and youth.

In November 2007, we organized a forum on educational policy and invited former and current CPS employees who advocate public military schools. At this forum (held at a university) they appeared to backpedal from the raw ugliness of the image, and the reality, of Chicago's youth of color being disciplined in public military-run schools. With folksy, generous voices and attempts to trigger laughs, they worked double-time to assure the audience that military schools were "just like regular CPS schools," and that the military focus was simply a "hook" to keep students in school. After the forum, an attendee (and a smart pal) commented, "If pole dancing brought in the students, and increased graduation rates, would CPS offer pole dancing classes?" While perhaps an ungenerous analogy, one that would chafe military personnel and sex workers alike, CPS and the city's refusal to take direct responsibility for making the radical public policy decision of letting the military make curricular and other choices affecting the lives of so many youth—a decision completely unsupported by evidence of its educational value for these students—is startling but hardly unpredictable.

And, in fall of 2008 we visited a local alderman who for years had been the head of the city council's education committee. Bolstered with fact sheets and our credentials, we stated our objections to public military schools. His response was that military schools were simply one option among many in the "boutique school" market. He parried our concerns, diminishing the role of the military in public schools with the by now well-established party lines emanating from CPS: these are not really military programs, they are school; parents and youth make choices, and nobody is forced to choose military schools; these schools have waiting lists, which proves that they are desirable; and so on. We left frustrated. Are these facts? In what way do facts matter, if at all? Somehow all the public and political conversations were organized to erase the real function of the military and the history of public education as civilian.

School "Choice" and the Consumption of Education

Across the United States, school choice is posited as a public response to an ineffective and bureaucratic public education system. Through choice-based reforms, parents are repositioned as consumers who must select the best educational option for their child. In Chicago, these choices—perceived by some as "depoliticizing" a system that is highly politicized, with ongoing wrangling over who will control the schools, their funds, and their jobs; CPS is the 2nd largest employer in the city and has an annual budget of over $5 billion ("Chicago's largest employers," 2008)—include local neighborhood schools, philosophic and thematic magnet and charter schools, and a range of selective admission academic preparatory schools, along with the newer military options. Choices, the logic insists, ensure quality through competition—as each school competes for each child, teachers will finally be induced to teach better, and the quality of all schools will subsequently improve (Plank & Sykes, 2003). What is public (money-sucking schools, slothful teachers) is cast as an artificial and wasteful monopoly, while what is private (quality through competition!) is presented as a natural and economical good (Lubienski, 2001).

School choice must be interpreted through larger economic shifts that have reframed the public sphere in the United States and subsequently altered the landscape for minorities. In the last thirty years, the prevailing bipartisan public sentiment has been to shrink big government—the de facto supporter of a public sphere—and this reconfiguration has translated into the contraction of assistance services and the inflation of punitive and surveillance functions. For some government agencies, the budgets may have grown, but the focus of each agency has shifted. For example, the enforcement arm of the Immigration and Naturalization Services (INS) has grown, but not the service or the assistance components (Bohrman & Murakawa, 2005, pp. 110–112). In fact, after 2001, the INS was aborbed by the new Department of Homeland Security. In the last thirty years, the budgets of the Drug Enforcement Agency, the Bureau of Prisons, and the INS have swelled at least 10 percent a year, while funding for social welfare programs (for example, housing subsidies, unemployment compensation, and food and nutrition assistance) decreased significantly since 1975 (Bohrman & Murakawa, 2005, pp. 110–112).

The neoliberal move to privatize what were once governmental functions in the United States started in the 1980s, with the Reagan administration's drumbeat of shrinking big government. Whatever the motivation, the rhetoric of smaller government typically translates into fewer public dollars for education, but more resources for the prison system (Blackmar, 2005; Harvey, 2005). This expansion of the punitive arm of the state and contraction of its welfare functions, and the subsequent privatization of public services (resulting in the faceless and unaccountable "market"-driving inequities), turns on the maintenance of particular tropes about race, gender, and sexuality.

Downsizing the welfare state is required because freeloaders and shirkers will take advantage of the state's generosity: this is the way the argument is often framed by conservatives pursuing a small government agenda; these types are present in mass media as lazy black mothers or illegal alien families although data illustrates that rates of welfare use at every socioeconomic level are relatively consistent across racial categories (Quadagno, 1994; Zucchino, 1999), and that "less than 1 percent of surveyed immigrants move to the United States primarily for social services" and "fear of deportation" and confusion about eligibility means that immigrants are less likely to use state resources (Bohrmann & Murakawa, quoted in Sudbury, 2005, p. 119). Concurrently, the privatization of public schools and outsourcing of education and discipline to the military trades on similar practices of scapegoating and the construction of particular identities as dangerous and a wasteful allocation of public resources. For example, privatized schools such as charters and those operated by for-profit and nonprofit agencies that hire employees with yearly contracts as instructors are represented as necessary because teachers hired by traditional schools are protected by tenure and unions, and military-themed schools are portrayed as essential because urban youth of color are undisciplined, unruly, even dangerous, and need to be controlled (Quinn, 2007; Lipman, 2004). These cultural imaginings—of who cannot be trusted, is dangerous, and is unworthy of care and support—are gendered, sexualized, and racialized and are deeply embedded in U.S. narratives (Hancock, 2004; Winant, 2004). With the repetition of these stereotypes, lies eventually become public truths, or the kind of "unitary and coherent" good sense that demands form (Gramsci, 1971, p. 328).

Using scapegoats to reshape the public sphere is an old tactic in the United States: Demonizing recipients is one clear way to call into question the legitimacy of a public institution or program and to assert the importance of market-driven regulation and oversight. And inflammatory versions of queer lives and movements continue to play an active role in this reconfiguring of the public and the private. Alisa Solomon, writing for the *Village Voice* on the 1997 "sex panic" triggered by an annual women's studies conference, Revolting Behavior: The Challenges of Women's Sexual Freedom, at the State University of New York, New Paltz, suggests: "'Where there is scant support for your campaign to downsize public institutions, seek out the sex—especially when it is female and gay'" (Arenson, 1997; Solomon, quoted in Duggan, 2004, p. 31). Homophobia and misogyny, frequently intertwined, are embedded within racialized discourses used to delegitimize those who use public in-

STRAIGHTENING UNRULY BODIES

stitutions. For example, single mothers on welfare are told that they need to get married ("Bush welfare plan," 2002), and the (primarily male) youth, nearly all low-income, and often Latino and African American, is targeted for enrollment in Department of Defense (DOD) schools because it is believed that they need military-style discipline and "strong male role models"—both positions are de facto anti-women and anti-gay.

Chicago as Ground Zero for Conscripted Students and Constricted Queers

In 2001, Chicago's Mayor Richard M. Daley, in a letter to the editor, commented approvingly on an article in an online journal, *Education Next*, in which then-Mayor of Oakland, California, Jerry Brown, offered his rationale for public military academies. Daley congratulates Brown's efforts to open a public military high school in Oakland and explains his own reasons for creating military schools in Chicago:

> We started these academies because of the success of our Junior Reserve Officers Training Corps (JROTC) program, the nation's largest. JROTC provides students with the order and discipline that is too often lacking at home. It teaches them time management, responsibility, goal setting, and teamwork, and it builds leadership and self-confidence. (Daley, 2001, ¶3)

Today, Chicago has the most militarized public school system in the nation, with the public school systems of other large and largely black and brown urban centers in the United States (including Philadelphia, Atlanta, and Oakland) following closely behind (Tugend, 2005). Nearly 10,000 students in Chicago participate in JROTC programs, beginning as early as middle school with the Cadet Corps, and another 2,400 are enrolled in one of Chicago's six public military high schools and military schools-within-schools (Banchero, 2007; Area 26 & JROTC Fact Sheet, 2007). Chicago is the only city in the nation to have academies representing all branches of the military (Banchero, 2007). With a war with no end in sight and declining recruitment numbers, it is no surprise that the U.S. military is attempting new recruitment strategies (Alvarez, 2007). As a logical part of that campaign, using dubious and often false promises—of enormous cash signing bonuses or free college tuition, free "first-person shooter" video games, and seemingly unfettered access to places children congregate without the presence of parents or guardians—the military is enhancing its youth-recruitment activities and targeting public education (Medina, 2007). In fact, as military recruiters across the United States continue to fall short of their enlistment goals—a trend spanning a decade—and as the number of African American enlistees, once a reliable and now an increasingly reluctant source of personnel, has dropped by 58% since 2000 (Williams &

Baron, 2007), the Department of the Defense has partnered with the Department of Education and city governments to sell its "brand" to young people and to secure positions of power over the lives of the most vulnerable youth.

Chicago's public military academies (along with other schools offering limited curriculums such as vocational education schools, Education-to-Careers Academies, and schools using only scripted Direct Instruction lessons) have been placed primarily in low-income communities of color, while schools with rich offerings (including magnet schools, regional gifted centers, classical schools, IB programs, and college prep schools) have been placed in whiter and wealthier communities, especially in the northside, along the lakefront, and in gentrifying areas (Lipman, 2004). In other words, it's no accident that Senn High School, with open enrollment, and a largely poor and immigrant student population, was forced, against the wishes of the school's principal, teachers, parents, and students, to house a public navy academy, while the selective high school, Northside College Prep, only a short distance away, was not.

Mayor Daley and others promote military schools by tapping into racialized fears when they describe the needs of some youth, but not all, for discipline and order. A sixteen-year-old student at the naval academy in Chicago seems to respond to these social perceptions when she says, "When people see that we went to a military school, they know we're obedient, we follow directions, we're disciplined" (Banchero, 2007, p. 16).

Just as Daley needs and uses fear and stereotyping to sell military schools, military schools and programs need and use the ideological constructs, if not the actual bodies, of queers and girls as the shaming contrasts against which youth soldiers will be created. Discipline, in these schools and programs such as JROTC, is constructed through the development of a rigid masculinity that is both misogynist and homophobic—soldiers aren't sissies and they aren't pussies either, although these terms and others like them are used to regulate behavior in military settings. "Almost every day of my junior year," one former JROTC cadet officer candidate reported about his experience with the program in high school, "I was made to do push-ups...I cleaned the commandant's office, I drank chili pepper-infused water, I ate lunch underneath a table, I had to wear a dress, and I was regularly called 'stupid,' 'maggot,' 'faggot'—all the happy, daily indignities that one had to suffer for the sake of 'military discipline'" (Wily Filipino, 2003). In Chicago, DOD schools and programs state that they conform to the city's antidiscrimination policy that includes sexual orientation, not to the military's Don't Ask, Don't Tell policy. Yet, the body does matter: The limp-wristed potential girl lurking just inside every male-sexed body, paired with mandatory hyper-normalized gender roles, are the ideological foils upon which the unruly body is straightened (straitened) into a soldier.

Historically, military socialization has been achieved through psychological conditioning that depends on threats of (and actual) physical violence and insulting evaluations of a conscript's sexual identity and masculinity (see Eisenhart, 1975; Johnson & Goldberg, 1995)—and both are seen consistently across decades. Examples from a Marine boot camp in the 1970s show that what starts in JROTC persists through enlistment:

> Aggression and...dominance were equated with masculinity. Recruits were brutalized, frustrated, and cajoled to a flash point of high tension. They were often stunned by the depths of violence erupting from within themselves. Only on these occasions of violent aggressive outbursts did the drill instructor cease his endless litany of "you dirty faggot" and "can't hack it, little girls?" (Eisenhart, 1975, p.16)

> In boot camp one recruit had...difficulty keeping up with the rigorous physical regime.... He was slender and light complexioned, not effeminate by civilian standards, but he was considered so in boot camp. He was continually harassed and called "girl" and "faggot."... The [Drill Instructor] looked at [him] and said, "you're a weak no-good-for-nothing queer," then turning to the glowering platoon, "As long as there are faggots in this outfit...you're all going to suffer"... "Unless you women get with the program, straighten out the queers, and grow some balls of your own, you best give your soul to God because your ass is mine and so is your mother's on visiting day." With a roar 60–70 enraged men attacked [this recruit], knocking him to the ground and kicking and beating him. (Eisenhart, 1975, pp. 16–17)

These cases illustrate how young people are turned into soldiers, but they also indicate how social norms (homophobia, misogyny) and military violence overlap, swap places, and are mutually infectious. In fact, the military has a lengthy track record of gender and sexual violence. In the last twenty years alone, some of the higher-profile incidents have included the 1996 admission that sergeants were regularly raping female trainees at the Aberdeen Proving Grounds; the testimonials of Beth Davis and other women who were sexually assaulted at the United States Air Force Academy in Colorado throughout the 1990s; the disclosures of many women in uniform (and private contractors) in Iraq that they have been raped, are afraid to use the bathroom at night for fear of sexual assault by their co-workers, and more (Harman, 2008; Houppert, 2008; Browne, 2007; Chen, 2008). Between 2004 and 2006, reports of sexual assault by the Department of Defense increased 73%; in 2007, 2,688 sexual assaults were reported to the DOD (Harman, 2008, ¶4). Yet relatively few of these are referred for courts-martial (the military version of criminal prosecution)—in 2007, only about 12% of sexual assaults were referred to courts-martial, according to DOD statistics; in California, by comparison, 44% of reported rapes result in arrests, and of those arrested, 64% are prosecuted (Harman, 2008, ¶7). Consider the testimony offered by Cassandra Cantu, on January 29, 2008, at a public meeting at Northeastern Illinois University, in an attempt to halt the implementation of "military studies" Reserve Officer Training Corps (ROTC) classes at the university.

> I served in the United States Air Force from August 2001 to August 2007. I joined the military for the same reasons many young people do. My recruiter promised me two things, that I would get money to go to school and that I would learn discipline. He wasn't lying. But unfortunately those both came at a cost. Discipline it turns out is about learning to be quiet and about not speaking up when you see something wrong. I learned this well. While in Afghanistan in 2006 I saw women being sexually harassed daily, and no actions were taken to challenge this blatant sexual harassment. When I voiced my concerns to leadership I learned quickly that my comments were turned against me. I was labeled weak and naive and told to suck it up; I was in the military and this is the way things are. I became afraid to walk into the gym or the chow hall because of what I like to call the "fish bowl effect." I would feel as if I had dumped a plate of food on my chest and everyone was looking. You could not go anywhere without sexually perverse comments.
>
> At a meeting one night my commanding officer told us about how individuals were using illegal drugs and illegally consuming alcohol on base. He was detailed in what punishments would be brought down on any individual caught doing either. Then he made a short reference to some "possible" rapes that were occurring on base. There was no mention of any action that would be taken against someone who committed this act. Nor was any information given on the circumstances surrounding these "possible" rapes. That night at dinner my CO sat across the table from me and I asked him about the rapes, wanting to know for the safety of myself and the two other females in my unit. He laughed with a joker smile on his face and said how he just couldn't understand how anyone could get raped if they carry a weapon 24 hours a day. He then turned back to shoveling food in his mouth. Several weeks later while walking to the latrines in the middle of the night I was sexually assaulted outside. Fortunately I was able to break away and find safety in my barracks. And I never reported it. Why would I? Who would believe me anyway, wouldn't it be simply dismissed as a "possible" attack? My leadership taught me to stay quiet. I was disciplined.
>
> But I refuse to be quiet now. My experience is not unique. I will not silently watch the Army ROTC come into our school and teach this type of "discipline" to my fellow students. Our university is proud of its diversity—including gender diversity—so why should we allow an institution on campus that shows such absolute disregard for the human rights of women? (Cantu, 2008).

We haven't even addressed the sexual assaults by members of the military on women and men in other nations—the Philippines, Japan, and more (Enloe, 2000). And, of course, there's the now-infamous "sexual torture scandal" of Abu Ghraib (Puar, 2007). The military, despite its history as an affirmative action employer and one of the first government branches to desegregate, continues to deny and minimize this epidemic of gender/gendered violence, from the "feminizing" and abuse of men, to the rape of women. And, in fact, violence—always a threat, even when not enacted—is a central component of the official *Don't Tell* policy for queers.

Moral Rot: Rooting Out the Fruits

Military training in schools has been used since the early 1890s as a way to regulate difference, with an initial emphasis on tracking toward race- and class-"appropriate" occupations and behaviors (Bartlett & Lutz, 1998). This push aligned with the prevailing political and economic interests of those in power, for example, white Southerners who supported black high schools on the condition that the schools would train black youth for work that did not compete with white labor, and for qualities (including "respect, obedience, and submissive acquiescence") that lessened the likelihood that these youth would demand equal treatment (Bartlett & Lutz, 1998, p. 121). After the start of war in Europe in 1914, there were more calls for universal military training in public schools and colleges as a way to resolve perceived social problems, including "moral rot" associated with increased national wealth, increases in the numbers of immigrants (who were seen as insufficiently loyal), and demands by labor, especially through strikes (Bartlett & Lutz, 1998). Proponents of military training in schools claimed that it would create better citizens and a "spirit of obedience, of subservience to discipline" (Anonymous, quoted in Bartlett & Lutz, 1998, p. 122). Pacifists and others who opposed this training were described as "moral syphilitics," a term that, together with "moral rot," evokes spoiled sexuality, if not the spoiled identity of queerness (Goffman, 1963).

The military and a militarized education were prescribed as a cure for "the hollow-chested boy" and the suspect masculinity of the immigrant, who could develop "a manly readiness" through participation in school-based drills and army training (Bartlett & Lutz, 1998, pp. 122, 123). Military education relies on the same fears at the core of the eugenics movement: that the "weakness" of the "white race," particularly its men and boys, was supported through the softening practices of public education, and by the moral unfitness of the "near white" immigrant populations whom boys would encounter in schools (Selden, 1999, p. b44). Eugenics, a white supremacist nationalist ideology that was actively advanced from around 1900 through the 1940s, shaped U.S. policies and perspectives into the 1990s; for example, Charles Murray and Richard Herrnstein claimed in *The Bell Curve* (1994) that immigrant groups tended to have lower IQ scores than whites for genetic reasons (Ordover, 2003). The movement forwarded the parallel ideas of "positive" and "negative" eugenics—the genetically superior should reproduce and the genetically inferior should not (Selden, 1999, pp. 54, 68). Queerness threatened the nation-state, and queers, along with others who would cause the degeneracy of the nation and race, including cross-dressers, race-mixers, and "hypersexual" women—in fact, anyone charged with physical and moral disability—were sterilized and even castrated toward eugenicist ends (Begos, 2002; Silliman & Bhatacharjee, 2002; Stoler, 1995).

Queers are still perceived as threatening and are still rooted out of our society and its institutions—schools, military, families, religion. In our organizing, it is the public silence surrounding the response to the "queer issue" in the military schools that resounds in the midst of all the other echoing silences about the move to privatize our public schools. In a context where military schools are offered as the educational choice for urban youth of color as a response to their posited disciplinary deficiencies, our attempts to include the issue of queer youth and staff in these schools (an argument that we perceived might possess traction with urban liberals) was completely ignored. The not-so-subtle message we received was that the "real issue" was the economic and racial draft of youth of color. But this misses the point. The privatization of the public sphere requires the production of specific identities; military schools need unruly youth of color to turn into soldiers and require both publicly sanctioned queer loathing and fear of black youth to shape up those boys.

Military schools, and the military overall, also attempt to conscript and narrow our queer resistances. DOD-run public choice schools are an issue for queers, not because Don't Ask, Don't Tell policies restrict the access of queers to full participation in the military, but because arguments for queers in the military require the active, systematic, and visible disparagement and destruction of queerness and queer lives, along with the tacit agreement that our limited participation in a diminished public sphere is more than acceptable, it is the only possible choice. Further, these schools are a problem for queers because they promote militarism to youth with public dollars, and they link white supremacy and poverty with homophobia and misogyny, as the bodies targeted for recruitment are primarily youth of color in working poor communities.

When gay and lesbian organizations focus on overturning Don't Ask, Don't Tell, they are essentially working to create access for queers to an obedient patriotism, arms-bearing, the free market, domesticity, and other forms of a diminished and fearful public sphere. In fact, DOD-run choice schools attempt to remap what our aims, as queers, should be—not rights to privacy and public life, and certainly not the right to life free from militarism; rather, we are offered only the normative choice of advocating for participation in a military that depends not only on poverty and racism but also on our revilement for its existence. This narrowed view of "queer issues" derails us from the goal of justice and should be rejected.

Rethinking Discipline: Artists and Queers in Every School

The links between militarized education, eugenics, racism, and nationalism are clear. In fact, calls for school-based or "universal military training" have been resisted and contested by parents and communities over decades. In 1916, Congress passed the National Defense Act, which approved the establishment of JROTC units in public high schools, and from the start its primary purpose was understood as ideological, not vocational (Bartlett & Lutz, 1998). The National Education Association took a strong stand against universal military training at its 1915 meeting but reversed its position later with a conflicted statement that "the training should be strictly educational...and military ends should not be permitted to pervert the educational purposes and practices of the school" (*Literary Digest*, July 22, 1916, quoted in Bartlett & Lutz, 1998, p. 124). Groups of parents, students, and educators resisted its imposition in widely publicized events. The *New York Times* articles "United Parents Vote against School Drill" (1929), which documents a parent group's unanimous vote against military drills in schools, and "Debate Military Training: School Pupils Give Views at Panel in Times Hall" (1945) offer a sense of the longevity of organizing against military training in public schools.

We have attempted here to demonstrate that in addition to using history to remind parents, youth, and politicians of the relationships between the military, gendered forms of violence, education, and eugenics, definitions and practices of discipline in education need to be expanded. In particular, we concur with a still-resonant 1916 essay in the *New York Times*, in which a school director, Dr. James Mackenzie argued, "If American boys lack discipline, by all means, let us supply it, but not through a training whose avowed aim is human slaughter" (Mackenzie, 1916, ¶16). However, it's important to note that many school-based routes to discipline, or practices toward expertise, offered to the children of the most privileged in society—art education (dance, music instruction, theater and performance, visual arts), sports and physical education, after-school activities and clubs from chess and debate to radio journalism, and much more—are not available equally to all youth. In Chicago, for example, 20% of principals report that their public schools offer no arts programming at all, with children in low-income communities of color less likely to have school arts than students in wealthier, whiter neighborhoods (Illinois Arts Alliance, 2005, pp. 3, 15). At the same time, it's increasingly clear that what seems like and is often touted as talent is actually a combination of time and access. As Malcolm Gladwell (2008) points out in his recent book, *Outliers*, it takes 10,000 hours and luck (read, the right family, the right birth-date, the right historic moment, the right connections) to become both su-premely skillful *and* successful. In short, when some youth are deprived of the arts in school, all of us are deprived of the ballads, the plays, the serigraphs they were *prevented* from creating. In agreement with Sennett (2008), that "making is thinking" (unpaged), the time is always ripe for more painting, knitting, and welding, and less testing in schools.

The educational policymakers in Chicago, primarily our mayor and his unelected school board and stream of appointed CPS CEOs, each as bad as the last, including, most recently, Arne Duncan (disappointingly picked by Presi-dent Obama to serve as secretary of education), could make decisions that support civilian forms of youth development; they could, for instance, put into place structures that develop young artists, designers, and scientists, not child soldiers. For example, what if, instead of expanding military schools, Chicago and the rest of the nation follows the lead of San Francisco's Board of Educa-tion, which in 2006 voted to eliminate JROTC programs from its schools through a several-year phase-out? "It's basically a branding program, or a re-cruiting program for the military," said one school board member before the vote (Tucker, 2006, ¶19). However, acknowledging that JROTC offered some desirable things to students and families, the SF board decided to develop and pilot new non-military-based programs to address those interests. San Fran-cisco's board subsequently voted that its public schools could not offer physi-cal education credit for JROTC programs, in a move predicted to "kill" JROTC in SF (Asimov, 2008). This is a strategy with promise; the SF board didn't just ask youth to accept the loss of a valued program but rather invited these students to tell them what they loved about JROTC and offered some good alternatives. And there are many other rich curricular and programmatic possibilities waiting to be articulated for our public schools.

We are wary, though, of the way niche schools, a primary form of "choice" plans, can be made to seem the only routes to rich, and even safe, educational environments. An example of this are the less-than-a-handful of national schools for queer youth (to our knowledge, only New York and Mil-waukee have such schools, Harvey Milk and Alliance, respectively). A pro-posal for a school aimed at LGBTQ youth and allies, initially called Pride Campus, was briefly supported by Chicago's Office of New Schools in 2008. The design team for the school included some well-connected public queer figures in the city, such as Dr. William Greaves, the Chicago liaison to the LGBT communities and Renae Ogletree, the director of student development for CPS ("Social Justice High School," 2008), but after the school attracted national publicity and opposition from Rev. Wilfredo De Jesus, "one of the most powerful evangelical ministers in Chicago," who teaches that homosexuality is "the work of the devil" and stated for the record, "What about that girl who is a virgin, who is being harassed by lesbians and gays to have sex, and yet you're going to build a gay school?" (Pupovac, 2008, ¶15, 17), the city refused to forward the proposal.

In an unsuccessful attempt to keep the plan alive, the school's design team renamed the school "Solidarity Campus" and expanded its mission to include all students facing bullying and harassment ("Board to vote," 2008). We are sympathetic to the concerns that prompted the school's planners and are fully aware, as teachers and as once-upon-a-time queer students, that schools can be frightening and dangerous places.[1] But we became educators, in part, to create schools that are not only healthy and safe places for all students, but also joyous, creative, and vibrant zones where all kinds of people encounter and learn about and from each other. We know that is possible and that it is public education at its best. From this perspective, the idea of a Pride Campus demands that we ask the following questions:

- With the advent of a Pride Campus, what happens to the queer and otherwise nonconforming kids left behind in all the other schools? Shame?
- Will Pride Campus let our school system continue to avoid ensuring that all schools respect and care for all students?
- Will schools push their trannies, fags, and dykes out to Pride Campus, rather than work with teachers, parents, and students to develop an inclusive educational culture system-wide?
- Is the school an admission of systemic failure to love our queer youth?
- Will the goal of safety for gender and sexual minority youth be best achieved through the establishment of one school or the enforcement of the city's already strong antidiscrimination policies?
- Can schools be made safer across the board, say, by repairing every broken window, boiler, and plaster wall, filling classrooms with art, plants, books, and computers, inviting neighbors to visit classes and plant school gardens, and strongly representing love and respect for every person in every building and community, so that all kids flourish?

It seems to us that Pride Campus, as a choice school playing to the fantasy that we are all individually responsible for our fates, neatly lets Chicago's public school system and administrators off the hook; if all queer kids can *choose* safety, albeit through isolation, why bother addressing the systemic issues of homophobia, gender normativity, and social violence? Further, the school, as proposed, is exclusionary, not because it requires high SATs or signed contracts for admission (it was going to be an open admission school), but because

---

[1] Our next chapter includes more information about school safety for queer students.

it asks for a declaration of identity/affiliation that many youth just can't make. The bottom line is that there will always be more queer kids in non-choice schools than in any Pride or Solidarity Campus, and the best way to ensure their safety is to seek every student's safety, and the best path to that is social justice.

If our nation has given up on the big job of building a society, or even a city school system, that actively recognizes everyone's rights, why should queers settle for a day campus as our safe zone? Instead, we propose thinking bigger: Let's declare every city a Pride *in* Solidarity Campus and then act like we mean it. We can start by seeking fully funded, fully public, fully arts-rich schools for all.

As we've indicated, increased and equally distributed resources are clearly necessary but not sufficient to address the deeper problems we have indicated here, including how school-based discipline is used to achieve normalizing, always anti-queer, ends, and how school safety for queers can't be achieved at the expense of school safety for all. What is needed are queer-centric, people-of-color-loving, and gender-flaunting definitions of discipline, and safety, too.

Teachers might begin with these activities: *design-and-sew-your-own-uniform seminars, gender-play AKA drag shows, weekly parades, baton-tossing teams, secret handshakes, clowning classes, daily dancing, feminist puppet shows, and, most important, history of social movement courses that remind us of and honor the justice-work of all who have gone before.* We need schools that link us to each other and to the most riotous and loving manifestations of our creative selves, through art, craft, and science that develop learners and creators, not child soldiers.

CHAPTER 2
"Lightning Rods":
Public Educational Policies,
the *Shadow State,*
and the Queer

put the LGBTQ into NCATE

your comfort, my silence

Fairness ≠ Justice

Red Campaign Stickers. Artwork by Keith Brown

*In early fall 2006, the National Council for the Accreditation of Teacher Educa-
tion (NCATE)—the primary accreditation agency for colleges and programs of
teacher education—asked for public feedback on proposed revisions to its "Professional Standards, 2002 Edition." The changes eliminated the phrase "social justice" and facilitated the de facto elimination of sexual orientation. We were
incensed at these removals but saw an opportunity in NCATE's invitation to offer
comments on the changes. As teacher educators and professionals, we felt we should
respond by pointing out the importance of social justice to education broadly—
specifically, how it was linked to this attempted erasure of queers through the re-*

moval of sexual orientation—and also wanted to ask our professional colleagues and organizations to support these observations or to supply their own. We drafted what we hoped was a professionally appropriate letter, on the assumption that this would be well-received by the organization, with assistance from Queer SIG members of the American Educational Research Association (AERA) and an anonymous and helpful contact within NCATE. Over 300 of our colleagues across the United States and Canada "signed onto" the letter, but AERA's president, Eva Baker, asked us to remove the names of any AERA-organizational entities who had asked to be represented (and there were several). Again following orders, we did this and then sent the letter off.

September 30, 2006

Dear Arthur Wise, National Council for Accreditation of Teacher Education (NCATE):

We call for the language "sexual orientation" and "gender identity" to be included in the main text of Standard Four: Diversity in the *Professional Standards for the Accreditation of Schools, Colleges, and Departments of Education, 2006.* As NCATE already acknowledges, teachers must be prepared for diversity in education, in their students, in their students' parents and families, among their teaching colleagues, as well as in class materials and discussions. Sexual orientation is a key part of diversity, as understood by our institutions and communities and as represented in the NCATE definition of diversity.[1] But the absence of sexual orientation and gender identity in the body of the standards, where other aspects of diversity are listed, sends the message that the needs and identities of LGBT students, families, and teachers are not important.

The following statistics indicate that addressing sexual orientation (a person's emotional, romantic, and sexual attraction) and gender identity (a person's sense of being male or female, feminine or masculine) in our schools is urgent[2]:

The population of lesbian, gay, and bisexual youth is large.

In a 2005 survey conducted by the Chicago Public Schools and the Center for Disease Control (the Youth Risk Behavior Survey) 6.6 percent of high school students attending Chicago Public Schools identified their sexual orientation as gay, lesbian, or bisexual.

---

[1] Diversity: Differences among groups of people and individuals based on ethnicity, race, socioeconomic status, gender, exceptionalities, language, religion, sexual orientation, and geographical area (National Council for the Accreditation of Teacher Education, 2006).

[2] The original letter contained 2003 data (6.3% identified as LGB) published in 2005; we've included the most current statistics here (Horn & Szalacha, 2007).

Schools are unsafe for lesbian, gay, bisexual and transgender (LGBT) youth.

According to the 2005 School Climate Survey conducted by the Gay, Lesbian, and Straight Education Network (Kosciw & Diaz, 2006):

- 67.1% reported that hearing "gay" or "queer" used in a derogatory manner caused them to feel bothered or distressed.
- 64.3% reported feeling unsafe in their school because of their sexual orientation.
- 45.5% reported being verbally harassed and 26.1% had experienced physical harassment in school because of their gender expression.
- 40.5% reported that teachers never intervened when hearing homophobic remarks.
- 18.6% reported hearing homophobic remarks from faculty or school staff frequently or often.

Negative school climates affect LGBT youths' well-being and academic success.

According to the 2001 Massachusetts Youth Risk Behavior Survey (Massachusetts Department of Education, 2002), LGBT students are more likely than the general student population to:

- attempt suicide (32.7% vs. 8.7%),
- skip school because they feel unsafe (17.7% vs. 7.8%).

Teachers are ill-equipped to confront issues that contribute to anti-LGBT hostility.

- 81.7% of LGBT students reported that they had never learned about LGBT people, history, or events in any of their school classes (Kosciw & Diaz, 2006).
- In a study of pre-service teachers, 57% indicated that they needed more training or education to work effectively with LGBT youth and 65% reported that they needed more specific education to address homosexuality in their teaching (Koch, 2000).
- In a study of high school health teachers, two-thirds indicated that they had inadequate education about LGBT issues (Telljohann, Price, Poureslami, & Easton, 1995).

Hostile schools and poorly informed, prejudiced educators clearly harm LGBT youth, but all students are hurt by homophobia and heterosexism in schools, including those with LGBT family members and those identified by others as acting outside traditional gender norms (Linville, 2008). Teachers must be able to create learning environments in which *all* children can be successful. All teachers must learn to:

- Create safer learning spaces
- Address anti-LGBT bullying and harassment in the classroom and school
- Communicate respectfully with all parents, including LGBT parents
- Teach students to respect the rights of others and coexist in a diverse world

Sexual orientation has never been part of the main text of NCATE's Professional Standards, but its inclusion in the glossary has encouraged educators to use NCATE's definition of diversity when planning how best to create and assess educational programs for teacher candidates. The proposed revisions direct readers to look at each standard for the elements of "diversity" to consider when creating and assessing teacher education programs. But sexual orientation is not included in any of the rubrics for any of the standards. This decreases the possibility that teacher education programs will include sexual orientation. Gender identity is similarly absent. Sexual orientation and gender identity should be stated explicitly in the main text of the Standard Four: Diversity, along with other categories like race, ethnicity, and socioeconomic status. Absence sends a message of non-importance.

Social justice, when used as a guiding principle, encourages recognition and inclusion; it seeks the presence of all community members. NCATE discredited its commitment to "help all students learn," when it removed social justice from the glossary of the Professional Standards. The elimination of social justice makes it even easier to marginalize sexual orientation and gender identity. And the elimination of the words "social justice" prompts the question: Who will be excluded next?

Luckily, examples of organizations that have taken ethical positions abound. Ontario's teacher accrediting organization vows that its members will "model respect for…social justice." The accrediting bodies of other professions, including the National Association of Social Workers, the American Psychological Association, and the American Bar Association, have explicit commitments to social justice and queer rights in their accrediting requirements. NCATE should, also.

Educators of conscience call on NCATE to establish and prioritize sexual orientation, gender identity, and social justice within our Standards.

Sincerely,
The Undersigned

The letter reached NCATE before its deadline for receiving "public comments." Then we waited…and waited.

We also forwarded the material to the email addresses of key members of our professional organization, the American Educational Research Association, optimistically hoping that this organization might take action. AERA's director of social justice emailed us to say that the organization was "aware of" the issue. Educational Researcher, *the journal of our professional association, refused to print the letter, stating that they published only scholarly research.* The Chronicle of Higher Education, *while helpfully supplying us with free website passwords— Sappho and Stein—but did not publish a shorter, zippier version.*

In February 2007, six months after sending the letter, we noticed that NCATE had posted a new set of revised standards on their website. Wise wrote that NCATE had added a definition and a new "professional disposition" for fairness ("fairness and the belief that all students can learn") to the standards. However, fairness is an inadequate replacement. Social justice connotes movements and people acting together; it aims at systemic change. Fairness, like personal responsibility or tolerance, is a term suited to the needs of those who wish to avoid conflict and can transform public policy issues into individual concerns.

As for AERA, we noticed that a column by Baker had been posted on the association's website, along with a statement titled "Key Policy Documents on Position Taking and Policymaking and Social Justice" (Baker, 2007; AERA, 2007). These documents revealed the process by which AERA will take action on social justice issues to be both arbitrary and capricious. For example, they stated that AERA will act only when issues are "monumental" and "sufficiently compelling," or of "compelling significance," or when issues are "compelling and fundamental" (AERA, 2007, p. 53). After reading the column and the policymaking article, we felt compelled to observe that AERA simply takes a comfortable "majoritarian" position—it will act only when a majority of members are concerned. But we wondered: Since when has social justice been defined through a popularity contest?

In response to the column by Baker and the revelation of the unanimous "down" vote on our letter's request to AERA, we called for action at its April 2007 meeting in Chicago, with a "RED Campaign." We asked all participants to wear red throughout the conference as a visible sign of anger at AERA's decision to remain silent and of our passion for justice. Our protest garnered immediate attention—the current, past, and future presidents of AERA together sent out an email to all members stating their commitment to diversity, including LGBT issues. The organization also hurriedly scheduled a private meeting with us, and a public meeting to air what it described as "both sides" of the issue. At the invitation of the RED Campaign, Bill Ayers, a professor of education at the University of Illinois, Chicago, spoke first, reminding us of the context of NCATE's deletions—war, scapegoatism, growing poverty, weakened rights. He called on AERA to push beyond bureaucratic constraints to act: "Whatever procedures are in place," he said, "we expect leaders to lead." His talk was powerful. And apparently, an older, straight, famous, white man was able to explain things in a way that the younger, unfamous female queers who called the action, and the 300-plus allies who participated in it, could not. Afterward, Baker thanked Ayers for "making the issues," finally, "clear." In fact, even before the meeting started, the NCATE representative invited Ayers to speak on the topic at the headquarters in Washington.

After Ayers concluded, the designated AERA representative elected not to speak, leaving the podium to NCATE's representative, Donna Gollnick, who stated that social justice had been removed because it was a "lightning rod" and a potential trigger for lawsuits. She denied the removal of sexual orientation but agreed with us, after the meeting, that revisions directing readers to use census categories might make it seem that way. She closed her talk by inviting feedback from AERA and its members. Many in the room added their strong statements to the public record, including a member of AERA's executive board, David Flinders, who described his vote for inaction as a mistake that he would do everything he could to correct. Baker and incoming president William Tate refused to state

that AERA would act. Tate did commit, though, to work on organizational procedures and transparency during his yearlong presidency.

Throughout the conference people in decision-making positions in AERA privately told us that they are fully "in support of the issues" (although few say the
words lesbian or even gay), but the public list of the reasons for inaction lengthens.
For example, we have heard that

- Sexual orientation is not an "official census category" and, therefore, can't be recognized.
- NCATE is too vulnerable in the current federal scene to support this initiative.
- AERA can't give feedback on another private organization.
- AERA is no longer a member of NCATE.
- AERA is a research organization and that this is not research.
- There is not "sufficiently compelling research" to support AERA taking a stand.
- AERA doesn't get involved in politics.
- We—Erica and Therese—do not represent any formal AERA entity.
- One of us is not even a paid member of AERA.

Most depressing is the not-so-subtle insinuation that the focus on SO/GI detracts
from other social justice issues—notably race—and that we were being "divisive"
by raising the issues of sexual identity and gender orientation. We are publicly
called out in several contexts as detracting from the more important social justice
work of AERA, in each instance by a powerful black woman in the organization. It
seems to us that fear motivates these responses, but the rebukes still sting. If there
are only a few seats for all of us "others," then there needs to be a new and much
bigger table.

And, as always, charges of "queer agenda" and "unprofessional" emerge. We
are two lesbians with agendas, not teacher educators with legitimate concerns. We
haven't done research, we are activists. Putting aside the question, What does research mean if it is continuously used in opposition to action, justice, communities,
and everyday work?, having our experience and expertise rendered invisible is frus-
trating and prompts other questions.

- How is it that in this moment of hyper-accountability for education the figureheads at the
  top of our professional organizations are so unaccountable?
- Why does a private agency with an unelected president and invisible procedures (NCATE)
  set the standards for our public education system?

By working to document the saga of our work, this chapter continues the discussion
of relationships between our profession and the privatization of public policies and
public education by tracing a brief history of NCATE and contextualizing it in a
period when the outsourcing of essential services emerged.

Privatizing Public Policy

Historically, teachers were "certified" by communities; no accreditation process existed (Tamir & Wilson, 2005). The main criterion for teachers was "moral values" and spiritual leaders vouched for the candidates (Tozer, Violas, & Senese, 1998, p. 59); these informal practices weeded out queer and other outsider educators (Blount, 2005). Vouching by spiritual leaders shifted to vouching by the state, and by the 1840s a majority of teachers in the United States received certificates from local officials based on an examination (Sedlak in Tamir & Wilson, 2005, p. 333). This allowed local control, but also the pitfalls of "patronage" and nepotism; schools varied widely in quality (Tozer et al., 1998). The state stepped into the picture, developing licensure requirements as a form of quality control over the growing numbers of women working in schools; throughout the start of the 20th century, state departments of education flourished and the first "normal" schools evolved into teachers colleges (Martusewicz, 1994; Tamir & Wilson, 2005).

NCATE was formed in 1954 by the American Association of Teacher Educators (AACTE) and four other educational organizations, including the National Education Association. By the 1960s, NCATE was the leading institution shaping teacher education. NCATE's power expanded in part due to alliances with state governments, and the move to standardize the teacher education curricula at the state level. For example, in 1999, the New York State Education Department mandated that all state schools be accredited by a federally approved accreditor or by the New York Board of Regents, and as NCATE was at that time the only federally approved accreditor, 58 institutions in New York moved to seek NCATE accreditation (Johnson, Johnson, Farenga, & Ness, 2005, p. 63). In Illinois, the Illinois State Board of Education (ISBE) has simply adopted NCATE standards for ISBE state-accreditation; any institution that wants to receive or maintain state accreditation must use NCATE standards. This process is hardly inexpensive. Reported costs for domestic accreditation range from $50,000 to $500,000 per institution (Johnson et al., 2005, p. 207); clearly, NCATE's federal approval and dominance is lucrative. NCATE maintains this prominence through marketing and brand development—its "brand" is affiliated with *Newsweek*—and strategic partnerships with state boards of education (Johnson et al., 2005, p. 19). NCATE, a nominally private, though functionally public agency, wields a great deal of power but remains virtually unaccountable.

NCATE, as a semi-public but opaque organization, is not an anomaly in education; as our previous analysis showed, the "public" is increasingly marginalized as bureaucratic and ineffective and is being replaced by a consortium of market practices that are perceived as more efficient or more natural than

the artificial monopoly. Along with the reduction of support for other "assistance" services, privatization means a loss of resources for elementary, secondary, and higher education, and an erosion (or an outright eradication) of the
institutions that make decisions, set standards, and shape policy for the entire
educational system. Today, foundations, nonprofit organizations, and some
for-profit entities form the shadow state, or the nongovernmental forces that
essentially fulfill what were once the purported functions of the state (Wolch,
1990; Gilmore, 2007). These structures "take responsibility for persons who
are in the throes of abandonment rather than responsibility for persons pro-
gressing toward full incorporation into the body politic" (Gilmore, 2007, p.
45). For example, both non-profit and for-profit sectors provide vital after-
school programming for families in a nation where welfare is out, and workfare
is in, and yet there is *still* no national child-care program. However, these
largely service-providing organizations generally do not also advocate for the
necessity of full, state-subsidized childcare. (These service agencies that make
up the shadow state are often staffed by women doing low-paying, non-union
jobs.) The shadow state does not have to be accountable to any public, just to
its unelected board members and invisible or too visible big-ticket donors. For
example, in 2006, Bill Gates was identified by the Education Research Center
in the report *Influence: A Study of the Factors Shaping Education Policy* as the
most influential person in educational policy in the previous decade, surpass-
ing George Bush (Swanson & Barlage, 2006). From education to public planning, since the early 1980s, this shadow state not only delivers central services
(from healthcare, and arts and museums, to education and housing) but is also
increasingly responsible for making fundamental alterations to "democratic"
institutions.

    NCATE, an organization with non-transparent policies and practices,
makes policy for our national system of public education: It sets the standards
that govern whether and which teacher preparation programs are accredited,
what teachers learn, and what and how our teachers teach. NCATE's power to
shape education locates the organization within the shadow state. Recent research illustrates that NCATE is less than lukewarm on addressing issues related to equity and justice in education (Butin, 2007; Pinar, 2006; Johnson &
Johnson, 2007). The litany of "pressing" educational issues that NCATE does
not take a stand on are numerous—abstinence-based education, corporal punishment, destructive federal policies, private for-profit teacher accreditation
entities, non- or segregated education of women in non-U.S. countries where
NCATE accredits teacher education programs, and more (Johnson et al.,
2005; Johnson & Johnson, 2007).

NCATE's definitions and dealings with its "diversity" standard also reveal its safe and functionalist approach. Rather than grappling with how the unequal and racialized distribution of wealth in our nation shapes the experiences of youth in public schools, NCATE uses "diversity" as a catchword for establishing that the organization helps foster the education of minority students (Johnson et al., 2005, p. 87), with quality taking second place to quantity. In fact, the most recent iteration of its standards define as "acceptable" only in-school experiences for candidates that allow them to work with "at least two ethnic/racial groups" (NCATE, Second Draft of Revisions, 2006). Yet, we wonder: Why did NCATE decide to stop there? If two are good, why not three? In this instance, NCATE's standards seem narrowing rather than broadening, and reductive rather than visionary. Further, removing social justice from the standards diminishes any need for the field to attend to the pervasive social problems that affect youth and their education—not only heterosexism, but also poverty, unequal funding of schools, and the factors that flow from these situations, such as fear, illness, hunger, and boredom and emotional trauma. However, rather than addressing these serious issues, NCATE has acknowledged it removed social justice because of fears that the phrase would attract negative attention from the right. At the U.S. Department of Education's National Advisory Committee on Institutional Quality and Integrity (NACIQI), Wise stated,

> I have come to learn, painfully over the last year, the term is susceptible to a variety of definitions...more recently the phrase has acquired some new meanings, evidently connected to a radical social agenda. So lest there be any misunderstanding about our intentions in this regard, we have decided to remove this phrase totally from our vocabulary. (Wise, p. 255, as quoted in Johnson & Johnson, 2007)

While NCATE may be under enormous pressure from social and economically conservative foundations and organizations (Butin, 2007), its acquiescence to this pressure underscores the problems we've outlined previously with shadow state organizations—they are not accountable to those whose lives they affect. Alternatively, strong public organizations with organized and educated members may also acquiesce to external pressure, but first there will be an opportunity for debate and a vote. In addition, if a national education organization is receiving pressure to become more conservative, imagine what kinds of pressures teachers and faculty are receiving across the U.S. policy-setting organizations such as NCATE. In addition, AERA can support educators in their quest to work for justice by foregrounding social justice in their policies and actions; backing away from including social justice organizationally leaves educators alone in their activist labors. Yet, although social justice is integral to education, it has never really been on the agenda for NCATE. Its removal from "official" documents is predictable and allows shadow state institutions to wield their clout silently and without public confrontation. And this is precisely why it should be countered. Social justice is a lightning rod.

Similarly, queer rights have never been on the agenda of teacher accreditation. In fact, the profession has a history of constructing queers as deviants who are "unfit to teach" (Blount, 2005). Max Rafferty, who in the 1970s served as California Superintendent of Public Instruction, and chair of the credentials commission in California that decided which teachers were morally fit to teach, stated: "And from the beginning, I do assure you, we took for granted the self-evident proposition that a homosexual in a school job was as preposterously out of the question as a heroin mainliner in the local drugstore" (as quoted in Blount, 2005, p. 142). Moving from these visibly and violently anti-gay sentiments, representations of statements and policies that proliferated in the 1970s, the anti-gay movement retooled their strategies in the '80s and '90s, and conceded the right to privacy for select queers, yet simultaneously restricted access to the public sphere.

> They defined privacy as a kind of confinement, a cordon sanitaire "protecting" public sensibilities. They attacked gay rhetorical claims for privacy-in-public and for publicizing the private, specifically, and worked to define the public sphere as an isolated, domestic site completely out of range of any public venue. (Duggan, 2003, p. 53)

"No Promo Homo" regulations further restrict the public, in the form of education funds, from being used to support positive discussions about queer sexualities in schools (Eskridge, 2000). This strategy of erasure and denial of rights in the public sphere continues to affect educators in direct and indirect ways. Queers may be mentioned by other social justice advocates when useful (as in the case of the military schools), and when not, they are often ignored. As with other high-profile topics, NCATE, not surprisingly, is uninterested in taking up the debate of queer inclusion in education.

A search (May 1, 2008) on NCATE's website for "sexual orientation" produced 86 "hits" for the term, most in definitions of diversity included in glossaries for versions of standards. But the term's inclusion in the definition of diversity is illustrational, not instructional. In fact, NCATE is careful to point out that aspects of diversity that must be addressed will be noted within each standard, and sexual orientation is not included in any of those. Queers are absent from the standards, and thus, will continue to be officially absent from public education, regardless of our presence in all areas of public life. The emergence of the strong shadow state in public policy arenas is delicate for queers and other non-majority marginals. Lacking mainstream support or rights, these populations can be easily erased in the non-transparent politicking of private foundations and other nonprofits as they craft services and policies. When there *is* support, in the absence of rights, it can be fickle. In the instance of NCATE and teacher accreditation, without the "tool" of sexual and gender identity-inclusive standards, and a democratic process, teacher educators will have a more difficult time advocating for that broader definition of diversity in their programs, as this professor of education notes:

> We will go through the accreditation process for the first time next spring (2008). The few of us faculty who are committed to diversity issues, including gender identity and sexual identity, were hoping...[the] process would help move our teacher education programs toward a social justice stance. However, without [the support of] NCATE, the majority of our (white, middle-class, heterosexual) faculty will end up maintaining (and reinforcing) the status quo. (P. Bullock, personal communication, February 20, 2007)

The accreditation processes of education stand in contrast to other fields, including psychology, law, and medicine, where accreditation is controlled by those fields and each profession's standards are developed by its members (Lugg, 2007). NCATE is not controlled by its membership; it uses the services of consultants from various educator organizations, a practice that effectively minimizes the influence of education's researchers and members of our professional organizations. This context has specific ramifications for queers, who have little-to-no federal clout or power. A membership-shaped accrediting process, such as in fields including law and medicine—the American Bar Association and the American Medical Association both have strong social justice and queer rights statements—might offer more representation of LGBTQ issues in the education profession, and could be one direction in which activists working on queer education issues should move (Lugg, 2007). We provide just a few examples of social justice policy leadership from a few other organizations below:

- American Bar Association (ABA) produced the 2007–2008 *Policy on Legislative and National Issues,* a document that summarizes the ABA's policy stances on a range of legislative, national, and professional issues including a call to "Support the enactment of laws and implementation of public policy that provide that sexual orientation shall not be a bar to adoption when the adoption is determined to be in the best interest of the child" (ABA, p. 183). It also "Urges Congress to create an independent, bipartisan commission to investigate and recommend the appropriate measures to rebuild the infrastructure of the Gulf Coast damaged by Hurricanes Katrina and Rita" (ABA, p. 186).
- The American Library Association (ALA), which sponsors local and national advocacy institutes to enable members to fight strategically to support a range of issues linked to public institutions, and literacy and well-being, is publicly opposed to the privacy violations of the U.S. Patriot Act, and educates and equips its members to organize against censorship (ALA, 2008).

- In 2007 the American Anthropological Association (AAA) voted to denounce the Human Terrain System (HTS), an initiative of the U.S. military that "embeds anthropologists and other social scientists in military teams in Iraq and Afghanistan." According to the executive board of AAA, the HTS "violates the AAA Code of Ethics, a code which mandates that anthropologists do no harm to their research subjects" ("AAA Opposes U.S. Military's Human Terrain System Project" n.d., ¶ 1).
- On August 19, 2007, the American Psychological Association adopted the "Position Against Torture and Other Cruel, Inhuman, or Degrading Treatment or Punishment and Its Application to Individuals Defined in the United States Code as 'Enemy Combatants'" in an attempt to curtail the participation of licensed psychologists in CIA and other military initiatives that use torture and other unjust forms of punishment ("Reaffirmation of the American Psychological Association position against torture," 2007).

The 2007 annual meeting of AERA came and went and no one communicated with us. We asked Ayers to do a follow-up email and he received the message that all of our issues were being addressed. Minutes were published and these issues were never mentioned. We were not surprised. Then, in late 2007 we discovered three pieces of news via NCATE's website. Two received "official" announcements:

1.   *The President of NCATE—Arthur Wise—was retiring at the end of the year.*
2.   *The term "social justice" was now officially and permanently removed from the Professional Standards.*

The third item wasn't announced; the changes just showed up online:

3.   *Sexual orientation had been worked back into the diversity standard.*

Debating the merits of continued pressure on these organizations, we decided to claim success for the continuing inclusion of sexual orientation and Wise's retirement. While we toasted ourselves and our allies, mourned the "official" loss of social justice, and kept moving, this work makes us think about where and how to focus organizing and activism.

We started this work, not because we wanted to organize against AERA or NCATE, but because these are the professional organizations that we are affiliated with and AERA has power and should, we thought, respond to its members and NCATE's clearly wrong deletions. Our engagement with the issues became organizing because these entities did not respond, and seemed uninterested in pursuing topics related to LGBTQ lives and communities, while all evidence suggests that queer issues are important in education and central to social justice work. Yet, a year or two after near-daily work on this project, what has been gained? It is hard to assess. Perhaps some small shifts in AERA. Hardly the "demands" we had initially suggested—language and policy changes, transparency, more advocacy, and resource allocation. As we continue with letter writing, attending events, and following the minutia of NCATE and AERA's workings, we wonder, how relevant are these organizations, anyway? Is it worth it to spend time fighting over their policy language? What is really at stake? And what will be gained?

Given the emergence of the shadow state and the power of these nongovernmental entities to provide services and to shape public policies, we are convinced that pressure on organizations like NCATE and AERA is necessary because policies matter, and because it is important to continuously name the erasure of "democratic" structures. Still, this can't be the only focus of our work. Perhaps our best successes to date have been community building and self- and lateral education. Mobilizing to work against punitive structures that work to shame those that speak out against injustice, and to talk back to these "quasi public" organizations that effectively seek to privatize and trivialize our lives, humanizes those that resist. We were educated during this work by colleagues who joined us, spoke out, sent emails, and more. And, at all the meetings and events connected to the RED Campaign and other work on this issue, it was interesting to see the impact that our queer visibility had on other "members," professionals, and educators—who came to sit near us, or looked the other way; who wore red scarves and carried red umbrellas proudly, or explained away their red nail polish with, "I didn't even know this was happening!"; who offered to design websites and pay for printing, or told us that we should not be agitators but to "work within the system." This clarified for us the conviction that it is seriously *professional* and educational to act: resisting trivialization and dehumanization and erasure builds communities in many ways and this may be the most important reason of all to challenge persistent oppression in bureaucracies

Tuesday, February 20

5:30-7:30pm

**Jane Addams
Hull-House Museum
800 S. Halsted
Residents' Dining Hall**

FREE. Reservations required.
call **312.413.5353**
for more information please visit:
www.hullhousemuseum.org

Anti-Gay Pledges and Teacher Education:
A Dialogue about the Tensions Between Private Beliefs and the Public Good

with **Erica Meiners, Therese Quinn,** and **Kevin Kumashiro**

Illinois is home to several colleges with anti-gay pledges. In 2006 **Erica Meiners** and **Therese Quinn**, both professors of education, attended a public conference for colleges with teacher education programs on the campus of Wheaton College, a private institution. The school asks all applicants for admission to sign a Community Covenant that describes "homosexual behavior" as a form of "sexual immorality" which is condemned. Wheaton also prepares students for certification to teach in public schools. At the conference, **Quinn** and **Meiners** attempted to open up a dialogue about these tensions: Wheaton's students are asked to agree that homosexuality is the moral equivalent of "theft, murder, and rape." At the same time, the Wheaton College Teacher Education Program's Conceptual Framework states, "candidates learn to work effectively with all children and their families regardless of race, creed, religion, national origin, sexual preference, disabling condition, or capabilities." And finally, ALL teachers are charged with doing no harm as they teach and work with LGBTQ youth and families in public education settings. How do education students balance these contradictions? What is the law? How can public education ensure that vulnerable LGBTQ youth and families in public schools are protected? What roles can the Illinois State Board of Education, NCATE, and other professional organizations play in leading teacher education toward true inclusiveness?

Please join us to discuss these and other questions. **Kevin Kumashiro,** of the Center for Anti-Oppressive Education at UIC, will facilitate the forum.

Flyer for Forum at Jane Addams Hull-House Museum.

CHAPTER 3
Redlining for the Lavender Menace:
Covenants, Privatopias, and Restricting Undesirables

Was it "prophetic" or just a weird coincidence that it was Friday the 13th the day we drove to Evangelical College? We hadn't reached the campus yet, but we were feeling anxious as we drove and talked about our upcoming day at the conference of the Illinois Association of Colleges for Teacher Education (IACTE). Evangelical College, the private campus where this public conference was taking place, is a religious institution. The school requires all student applicants (as well as faculty and all other employees) to sign a "Community Covenant" that describes "homosexual behavior" as a form of "sexual relations outside the bounds of marriage between a man and a woman" that is thus considered "immorality" (Evangelical College, 2007, unpaged).

We weren't sure why the meeting of a public and at least theoretically inclusive organization was being held at a college with an exclusionary "faith statement," but we were already aware that this and similar schools in Illinois are accredited by the state to educate teachers. That knowledge inspired us to develop an "Accredit Love Not Condemnation" campaign to promote the position that teachers who condemn their students and their students' family members on the basis of sexual identities do not belong in public education. The campaign centered on an affirmation—the profession of teacher education should validate colleges and programs that aim to foster respect and love for all students, families, and teachers.

The conference was brought to order with a prayer led by an older white man in a business suit. The room fell silent, as most heads bowed and most eyes closed. The prayer began, "We just thank you, Jesus."

Afterward, during a breakfast and networking time, we circulated, passing out pink fist-inside-apple buttons and copies of the pledge and explaining our campaign—we were wearing T-shirts with the Accredit Love slogan, which prompted questions and discussion. Many people pinned the buttons to their shirts; as they moved about, these pink dots punctuated the space. But an equal number of our colleagues wouldn't make eye contact with us; they listened quietly, asked few questions, and seemed to be hoping we'd move away from them quickly. We placed copies of this pledge on each table:

ACCREDIT LOVE NOT CONDEMNATION

Teachers need to be well prepared to teach all students. Teacher education programs should support candidates by preparing them with the information and experiences they will need to teach and work with LGBT youth and family
members. All teachers are responsible for gaining the education they need to teach
and advocate for the well-being of LGBT students. All teachers should respect
LGBT students, LGBT family members, and the identities and histories of
LGBT people in classrooms and elsewhere. I pledge to do so myself. This retracts
any earlier statements to the contrary.

Sincerely, _____Date _____

*A few people handed us back signed pledges right away, but unsigned copies
littered tables throughout the conference, despite the presence of a number of other
gay and lesbian participants. During the first break, one of us visited the restroom
and was followed there by a woman who whispered, "Here," while holding out a
signed pledge. This encounter felt furtive and shaped by shame so powerful that it
wouldn't allow a public return of the signed paper.*

*Next, Sharon Robinson, the CEO of the American Association of Colleges for
Teacher Education (AACTE), the conference's parent organization, spoke. We
had, so far, been working around the edges of the conference. But now, one of us
stood and asked, "Will AACTE support calling for the inclusion of social justice
and sexual orientation in NCATE's diversity standard?" Robinson answered with
a long, rambling, and deflective speech about respect and professionalism and
made no mention of lesbian and gay students and their families, or about sexual
orientation more generally. Social justice was just as absent.*

We left the conference with four signed pledges.

*A month later, one of us was told by her associate dean that Evangelical Col-
lege was going to vote on whether or not to "censure" us. Shortly after that, we
each received a letter from Evangelical College informing us that our behavior at
the meeting was inappropriate, our interpretation of their community covenant was
faulty, our approach showed a bias against "traditional Christianity," and our
action at the conference was surreptitious and unprofessional. If we did not apolo-
gize, the letter said, Evangelical College would report us to our "respective superi-
ors." We responded with a letter that addressed their points and invited them to co-
host and organize with us a public forum on "Private Beliefs and the Public
Good." We wrote,*

For us, and the queer youth, teachers, parents, colleagues and allies we work alongside,
the Accredit Love Not Condemnation action…was a great success. We distributed
love-centered flyers and pink teacher-power buttons. These, along with our positive
queer presence, countered Evangelical College's gay-excluding policies. As importantly, we raised questions about the appropriateness of Evangelical as a meeting place

for the professional organization of teacher educators in Illinois, and the importance of sexual orientation and gender identity as key aspects of diversity. We believe that [this organization] should not legitimize with its presence any institution that dehumanizes and devalues lesbian, gay, bisexual, and transgendered people. Evangelical's "Community Covenant," which is part of the application for admission to the college, equates "theft, murder, and rape" with "homosexual behavior." As lesbians, educators and as citizens, we find this an insulting and dangerous comparison, and the kind of assertion that lays the ground for violence against LGBTQ people. In addition, for queer youth, families and educators, the distinction you attempt to make between identities and acts is false and cruel. Sexuality is not divisible from other aspects of our lives as workers, parents, and students; no person should have to agree to forgo loving relationships in order to be safe from hateful characterizations.

It is hard for us to understand why you think the Accredit Love Not Condemnation project shows a "clear bias against traditional Christians." It is inspired by and grounded in the traditions of critique and resistance exemplified by many Christians at the forefront of the profession of education including Margaret Haley, organizer of the first American teacher's union in Chicago; Myles Horton, co-founder of the Highlander Folk School who played an integral role in the labor and civil rights movements; and Paulo Freire, author of *Pedagogy of the Oppressed*. Outside this field, Christians have been central to worldwide movements against oppression. The list is nearly endless, but includes Harriet Tubman, John Brown, Eleanor Roosevelt, Jane Addams, Desmond Tutu, James Baldwin, Óscar A. Romero, Fannie Lou Hamer, Bayard Rustin, Cornel West, and Mel White. We claim their engaged faith traditions as our guides.

We disagree with your letter's claim that our distribution of the Accredit Love flyers was "surreptitious." In addition to writing our email addresses on the flyers, as your letter notes, we walked from table to table during the meeting breakfast, passing out and explaining the flyers; wore T-shirts with the same slogan; introduced ourselves to the conference and individuals; and passed out business cards. However, secrecy is a strategic tactic that is respectable and sometimes necessary—the Underground Railroad is a clear example of this—and one that should be familiar and acceptable to Evangelical, which highlights a rich history at the forefront of the abolitionist movement on its website. But, we didn't choose secrecy for this campaign; we chose visibility to counter the shame and silencing that institutions like yours seem to prefer for queers.

We also reject your characterization of our distribution of the Accredit Love flyer as "unprofessional." Sexual and gender minority youth are unremittingly subject to violence and hostility in public schools, and we believe it is our professional obligation to raise this issue and seek solutions with our colleagues in teacher education, despite the desire of some to suppress that dialogue. It is the responsibility of the profession of teacher education to affirm and advocate for all students, parents and teachers, including those who are queer. Advocacy requires that problems are made visible. And that is what we have attempted to do.

We regret that you found the Accredit Love Not Condemnation flyers and pledge "quite distressing." However, imagine how we felt to discover that our profession held a meeting on a campus where every person has sworn that the expressed sexualities of LGBTQ people, including youth and teachers, are the moral equivalent of "rape and murder"? Distressed is the mildest way to describe our reactions: pain, fear, and anger are more accurate. Public meetings should not be held at institutions that degrade and exclude entire classes of people.

We appreciate and accept your invitation to talk further and propose co-hosting a discussion about this topic—Tensions Between Private Beliefs and the Public Good in Teacher Education—in a public venue, with fellow teacher educators and students of education and members of LGBTQ communities. We've secured a site, the Jane Addams Hull-House Museum, and a tentative date and time, Feb. 20, from 5:30–7:00. We suggest that we work out other details together—who to invite, how to organize the dialogue, food or not—if you choose to participate. If not, we plan to hold the discussion anyway, and hope you will announce the event to your students and staff. In particular, we would like to invite your LGBTQ students, staff and faculty to attend.

Sincerely…

While we effectively countered the shaming strategy intended to privatize the issues—posing them as our unprofessional lesbian agenda—and invited our colleagues to a public dialogue, this experience and its aftermath makes us think of the many ways that the state supports exclusion. We received no response to our letter, and although we received emails from an Evangelical faculty member who wanted to meet us to talk, in private, in a coffee shop, our invitation to participate in a public dialogue was not acknowledged.

We held the event, "Tensions between Private Beliefs and the Public Good in Teacher Education," in a public venue, without representation from Evangelical College. We followed up this public event with a letter to IACTE requesting that all meetings be held at venues that comply with Illinois's antidiscrimination language. This letter resulted in a flurry of formal and very polite correspondence. We were told that we could not write a letter requesting the IACTE to change their venues, only the respective "heads" of our organizations could. We made these requests, and first Therese's "superior," Drea Howenstein, sent a letter, and after a few months of silence her next rotating chair (these positions are held by all tenured faculty for three-year terms), John Ploof, followed up with a letter requesting that

no future conferences or events of the Illinois Association of Colleges for Teacher Education be held on campuses whose codes of conduct do not comply with state anti-discrimination law.

Erica requested that her union—University Professionals of Illinois (which represents a number of faculty at universities in Illinois)—also send a letter, but despite an initial agreement from the diversity committee of her union, the letter did not appear. The IACTE responded to Ploof, informing him that the SAIC was not a "member in good standing" (although the school had been attempting to make payment for weeks and was in communication about the issue with IACTE) when this request was made, therefore, regrettably, they could not act on this request.

Ploof was told by the president that her term was ending (we imagined her relief) and that the incoming president would take up the matter by putting it on the fall 2008 agenda. Fall 2008 came and went, and Ploof wrote the new IACTE president asking for an update and some action. Spring 2009 is now looming, but there has been no response.

Throughout this process, we struggled to identify the role of the state. Whose responsibility is it to accredit teacher education programs? Why does the State Board of Education use standards developed by a quasi-public but unaccountable organization? What is the relationship between a private college and the public function of training educators to work in public schools? To whom do we direct our questions about exclusion? Investigating these questions reveals the deep U.S. history of interrelated and state-endorsed exclusionary practices and private market forces. Often invisible, but notoriously not always, state-sanctioned and "private market"-excluding practices are deeply entrenched in the United States and have entangling connections to two of the pillars of American identity—free speech and individual rights.

Redlining, Covenants, and Histories of Exclusion

Institutionalized respect for "private" agreements and processes that restrict access has played an important role in the intertwined histories of housing and educational policies. Specifically, redlining and restrictive covenants, covenant-controlled communities, and community covenants or "belief" statements such as Evangelical's are all linked through their goals of controlling access to resources and expression; each of these works not only to literally block the free movement of bodies in space, but also to prevent some individuals from being understood (and able to act) as fully human. In this section, we provide a short overview of the history of discriminatory tracts in housing and their contemporary manifestations, and because residential policies are intimately linked to educational policies, we also point to the parallel establishment of exclusionary "segregationist academies" and the mechanisms that have enabled private educational institutions with discriminatory covenants to flourish. When the public sphere expands to include people with new practices that challenge dominant ideologies—for example, African Americans integrating politics and neighborhoods during Reconstruction—those opposing such changes deploy new institutions and rhetoric, from laws and oaths, to schools and organizations, that work to enforce their status quo.

Restrictive covenants based on race and religion, or agreements between buyers and sellers of property to exclude specific groups (African Americans, Jews, Chinese and Japanese immigrants, Filipinos, Mexicans, or any non-whites) from future ownership, flourished in the post-Reconstruction period—

1890 to the 1930s. This era is referred to as the "Nadir of [U.S.] race relations"; during these years, violence was used to drive people of color from
communities across the United States (Loewen, 2005, p. 25; Turnbull, 2005;
Jones-Correa, 2000–2001). In response to a nationwide series of attacks on African Americans (misleadingly called "race riots") that took place between
1917 and 1921, the National Association of Real Estate Boards encouraged the
adoption of racially restrictive covenants to create segregated communities
(Jones-Correa, 2000–2001, p. 559). For white people, the way to address the
"race question" was to avoid it by creating all-white neighborhoods and towns
through local laws and private property agreements.

Restrictive covenants persisted until the Supreme Court decided in 1948
(*Shelley v. Kraemer* 334 US 1) that racial restrictive covenants were unenforceable, and the 1968 Fair Housing Act (FHA) invalidated them. However, the
FHA was defanged through inadequate funding, making it difficult to investigate and prosecute and thus inhibit the implementation of these covenants
(Lipsitz, 1998). Indeed, their proliferation was rendered nearly invisible, but
they are still commonly present in deeds. In 1986, William Rehnquist testified
before the Senate that he was unaware of the restrictive covenants in the deeds
of two properties he had purchased, one banning sale or lease to "members of
the Hebrew race" and the other to anyone "not of the White or Caucasian
race" (Oser, 1986, ¶14, p. 17); in 1988, George W. Bush purchased a home
with a deed that restricted its use to "white persons only"; and John F. Kennedy, Richard Nixon, Ronald Reagan, and George H. W. Bush also owned
property with racially exclusionary deeds (Gerber, 1999, ¶1).

Linked to restrictive covenants is redlining, a process through which "undesirables" are systematically restricted and excluded. Redlining is a practice
that dates to 1930, when the Federal Home Loan Bank Board established
"high risk areas" on its residential security maps by shading them in red (Kantor & Nystuen, 1986). This color-coding identified communities to financial
institutions as "high risk" neighborhoods "where loans were not to be made
because of [the] high concentration of black residents" (Kantor & Nystuen,
1986, p. 310). Integrated communities were a social "risk," therefore, they
were also an economic risk.

While the FHA banned overt discriminatory housing practices, covert
forms of redlining have been used to similar exclusionary ends, including
charging higher interest rates or requiring larger down payments in some
neighborhoods (Kantor & Nystuen, 1986). Real estate companies still "steer"
clear of or discriminate against non-white house purchasers and renters. National Fair Housing Alliance's (NFHA) 2006 report identified about "3.7 million instances of housing discrimination every year" (fewer than 1% are

reported) and "one of the most blatant findings of NFHA's 2006 investigation was the use of schools as a proxy for the racial composition of neighborhoods" where white families are steered away from neighborhoods with predominantly non-white schools. In 2005, NFHA "filed nine complaints against real estate companies in Atlanta, Chicago, Detroit, Mobile, AL and Westchester County NY. Seven of these complaints involve franchisees of the national companies of Coldwell Banker, Century 21 or Re/Max" and the majority of these complaints involved racial steering practices (NFHA, 2006 Report, pp. 2–3).

Redlining and restrictive covenants have had long-lasting effects on the authors' home city, Chicago. After a 1919 "race riot," covenants spread rapidly across Chicago; by 1947, racist covenants were in place in half of the city's neighborhoods, forming a barrier that effectively prevented African Americans from residential movement for decades (Massey & Denton, 1993; Jones-Correa, 2000–2001). Demographic maps of Chicago today show roughly the same pattern of racially concentrated communities as those that were present at the legal end of segregation. In 1980, Chicago was identified as "hyper-segregated"—that is, as one of the ten U.S. cities in which the average African American lived in a neighborhood that was at least 80% black (Massey & Denton, 1993, p. 160).

Redlining has also been used to eliminate other kinds of "undesirables." What we propose might be called "lavender-lining," for instance, has been used as a tactic by insurers aiming to exclude queers. Applicants perceived to be at risk of contracting AIDS, identified via zip codes and occupations (antique dealers, interior decorators, hairdressers, florists) thought to be associated with LGBTQ communities, were marked as uninsurable (Kantor & Nystuen, 1986; Li, 1996). Rather than explicitly tracking bodies, targeting "lifestyles" for exclusion and control is also the focus of contemporary restrictive covenants that address home and property upkeep and use; these rules are often associated with planned or gated communities and address everything from acceptable types of lawn grass and pets, to approved and banned housing paint colors (Risley, 1991). Proponents of these "covenant-controlled communities" portray the restrictions as neutral or beneficial. One administrator of a housing development charged with ensuring compliance said he prefers the term "'protective covenants'" and went on to claim that "'You have to give up something to get something...you're going to give up some personal freedoms. What you're getting is the knowledge that your neighbor isn't going to paint his house chartreuse'" (Risley, 1991, ¶33–34).

But rules that prohibit pit bulls or chartreuse houses also have racial and cultural valences. This can be clearly seen in the case of writer Sandra Cisneros, who was called before a housing board in 1997, when the color she chose to paint her home in San Antonio, Texas—purple—was found to be out of compliance with the community's requirement of "traditional" housing colors. About this event she wrote,

> I want to paint my house a traditional color. But I don't think it unreasonable to include the traditions of los tejanos who had a great deal to do with creating the city of San Antonio we know today... I thought I had painted my house a historic color. Purple is historic to us....It is present in the Nahua codices, book of the Aztecs, as is turquoise, the color I used for my house trim; the former color signifying royalty, the latter, water and rain...
>
> We have a tradition of bright colors. Dr. Daniel Arreola of Texas A&M University has written that in a survey of 1,065 houses in a Mexican-American district in San Antonio, 50 percent showed evidence of brightly painted exteriors....That passion for color is seen even now in our buildings on both sides of the border. Mango yellow, papaya orange, Frida Kahlo cobalt, Rufino Tamayo periwinkle, rosa mexicana and, yes, even enchilada red. This issue is not about personal taste, but about historical context. Why is it so difficult to concede a Mexican influence, especially when so many people of Mexican descent lived in the city? (Cisneros, 1997)

"Privatopias" or planned communities that "pursue utopian aspirations through the privatization of public life" have proliferated, at least in part, because they are perceived as less dangerous—they exclude everyone except "people like me" as if "like me" is an assurance of something very good (McKenzie, 2003, p. 4; McKenzie quoted in Wilson, 1995, p. A1). Like the "sundown towns" documented by James Loewen (2005), communities that were founded as all white or those that drove out their citizens of color, privatopias screen to achieve *sameness*, which is then translated as *safety*. Today's exclusions are gained without physical violence, but gated communities, and their developer and realtor promoters, evoke fear to maintain their borders. "Single women have unique needs," announces an article/advertisement for property in planned communities (Demographics, 2008); "the gated community makes me feel more comfortable and secure," and "[the community] is gated, which makes me feel safer," two satisfied purchasers are quoted (¶3,11). In 2006, developers in Texas and Kansas marketed new housing developments as "sex offender free," requiring background checks for all potential purchasers; if someone who lives in the communities is convicted of a sex offense, they will be fined $1,500 a day until they leave. The first wave of development, 150 housing units, in the Lenaxa (Kansas) community was sold out (Koch, 2006, ¶2).

Controlled communities like these are an increasingly popular segment of the housing industry, with over 50 million residents in the United States (McKenzie, 2008, ¶3). Cultural geographer Setha Low (2005) documents that "one-third of all new communities in Southern California are gated, and the percentage is similar around Phoenix, Arizona, the suburbs of Washington DC and parts of Florida" (p. 86). These planned cities are governed by private associations that frequently do the work that the state once did, including picking up the trash, organizing security, and maintaining the association's "common" property. Once public functions are now being absorbed and regulated by private associations, but these physical spaces and accompanying benefits are offered solely to property owners, within the limits of privately determined and non-negotiable "agreements"—in short, the spaces, functions, and rights once associated with the public space of citizenship are being shifted to the private space of goods and consumerism. Queers, who for the foreseeable future will be more often on the list of "undesirables" than other "people NOT like us," can hardly benefit from the increasing move to privately controlled space and the curtailed rights of "restrictive" space. The market rewards popularity and capital and aims to exclude everything and everyone else. "Likeness may be a criterion for membership in private organizations, but it can never be a requirement of belonging in a democracy" (Jakobsen & Pelligrini, 2003, p. 149).

From Private Housing to "Private" Institutions for the Public Good

Private associations and institutions with corresponding private and privatizing beliefs have been historically produced in direct relationship to civil rights struggles and changes in the public sphere. For example, when schools were "forced" to desegregate after the Brown decisions, "with all deliberate speed," in a strategy known as "massive resistance" that was initiated by Virginia's Senator Harry Byrd and authorized by the state's governor, integrated public schools were shut down or defunded (*Yale Law Journal*, 1973, p. 1437). In Prince Edward County, Virginia, public schools were ordered padlocked by city supervisors and remained closed for five years, from 1958 to 1964, until the federal courts ordered tax collection to begin again and for public schools to be opened (Saxon, 1995; *Griffin v. School Board of St. Edward*, 1964). In fact, most Southern states passed legislation that would allow or mandate closing schools that integrated, while at the same time creating means to support private segregation schools (Ryan, 2004).

Code terms for white supremacy, such as claims to *tradition* and the *right to individual liberty*, in the form of politically and structurally supported "freedom of choice" plans, were the hallmarks of these segregatory initiatives (Lipsitz, 1998; Ladson-Billings, 2004; Ryan, 2004, p. 1636; Lassiter, 2006). "Voluntary" private segregationist academies opened up across the south to cater to white children and to "private" beliefs held by white supremacists.

These schools were directly and indirectly supported by the government through tuition grants, the "transfer of facilities from closed public schools," and state and federal tax exemptions (*Yale Law Journal*, 1973, p. 1436; Andrews, 2002). Other resources and labor were provided by private economic, civic, and religious institutions such as the Baptist Church, banks that provided start-up loans, and local groups including Citizen's Councils and parents organizations.

> In South Carolina White citizens developed [private] academies as a way to avoid school desegregation. South Carolina delayed desegregation until 1963, when Clemson University was the first school in the state to desegregate. Some two years later on August 10, 1965, the South Carolina Independent School Association (SCIA) was founded with 7 schools. Today, SCIA comprises 90 schools with 28,000 students. South Carolina is also home to a private Christian school association that includes more than 100 schools. (Ladson-Billings, 2004, p. 7)

As this observation by Ladson-Billings indicates, private segregation academies and Christian private schools are linked: the "most significant and enduring" of the private schools that were founded to avoid integration were the Christian academies or Christian day schools initiated by evangelical Protestant sects and nonsectarian Christian churches (Ryan, 2004, p. 1637). In an ironic turn, in recent years segregationist Christian academies, faced with declining enrollments, have sought and become increasingly popular with African Americans; black private school enrollment has been growing faster than overall private school enrollment, with Christian schools, many previously all-white and with supremacist origins, getting the largest share of this population (Dent, 1996). Urban education scholar Jacqueline Jordan Irvine notes that "a lot of things that go on in these schools…resonate with many African American parents and African American tradition…. There is a sense of order and discipline. Segregated black schools were highly disciplined and highly structured schools and a lot of older black teachers were teaching religion and values" (quoted in Dent, 1996, ¶10). While these qualities of order and value congruence may make the schools appealing to black families, there have also been reports of conflicts occurring with the demographic shift, as African Americans call for culturally inclusive curricula and point out racism, such as the teacher and administrative discomfort with interracial marriage at the Indiana Christian Academy reported by a black student who subsequently chose to leave the school (Dent, 1996).

Racially exclusionary educational practices, including calls for segregationist dating, have not been confined to K-12 institutions. Public institutions in the south, such as the University of Mississippi in 1962, desegregated, after race riots, under the presence of federal troops. For private postsecondary institutions, the process was slower. In 1970, the Internal Revenue Service (IRS) declared that private institutions claiming federal tax exemptions must comply with federal antidiscrimination standards. Perhaps the most visible case is Bob Jones University (BJU), which agreed to admit African American students in 1971; yet until 1975 all African American admitted students were required to be married. The IRS revoked the university's tax-exempt status in 1976, because of its ban on interracial dating; although BJU tried to challenge this revocation (and received support for that endeavor from the Reagan administration) in the Supreme Court, the *university elected to forgo its tax-exempt status rather than permit interracial dating.* The university's prohibition against interracial dating was not lifted until 2000, but the school has not reapplied for federal tax-exempt status. And although it now avoids condemning interracial romance, it has no apparent compunction about its ban on same-sex love. In fact, in letters sent directly to former students in 1998, BJU announced that it would have gay alumni arrested for trespassing if they attempted to visit the campus, though the school later said that queers could still visit the BJU museum so it wouldn't lose its tax-exempt status, held independently from the school ("Bob Jones University Tells Gay Alumni," 1998). This track record of exclusion and banning has not hurt the school—BJU is not marginal; it is accredited by the Transnational Association of Christian Colleges and Schools (TRACS), which is recognized by the U.S. Department of Education and works with over 100 institutions across the states, according to the school's and the organization's websites (TRACS is a voluntary, nonprofit, self-governing organization of Christian postsecondary institutions). Further, BJU is a well-known pit stop for Republican presidential nominees and candidates, including Ronald Reagan, Bob Dole, Alan Keyes, and George W. Bush (Carlson, 2005).

The historic modes of restriction we have been discussing—exclusionary covenants connected to sexuality, red- (lavender-) lining, or identifying queers for the purpose of elimination—come together in education. Just as "maintaining tradition" was used as a code phrase when segregationist academies were created in the years after the Brown decisions, now the term is used to justify anti-queer educational institutions. Legally, the rights of LGBTQ students in schools are not as clear as those of racial minorities. Sexual identity is not a protected federal category, and private schools like BJU along with other private institutions, such as the Boy Scouts, are free to ban expressions of queer desire and love as well as, unavoidably and quite purposefully, the bodies that do that desiring and loving (Zehr, 2006). In these private schools, speech and expression are regulated through the lack of employment protection and unionization for all staff. Far from "free," each is a gated community and a sundown town for queers, who can be excluded, who must remain in shadows, and from whom silence is required. But public education is also, and perhaps increasingly, restrictive for queers.

No Speech Is Free

Our actions at Evangelical, as in our work explicated in previous chapters, were prompted by a sense that our profession should visibly engage with urgent civic issues such as the following: Should private colleges with discriminatory "covenants" be supported (accredited) by the state to produce teachers for public schools? Should public organizations hold meetings at private campuses that discriminate? How do discriminatory policies—such as Evangelical's—contribute to the dehumanization of LGBTQ bodies in schools? For us, these appeared to be *obvious* tensions and questions, yet when we raised these questions to colleagues in our profession, the response was often silence; some of our allies asked what we perceived as equivocating counter-questions:

- *What about free speech?*
- *Is an action such as signing a pledge really an indication of a belief?*
- *As private institutions, don't they have the right to privacy and to private beliefs?*
- *Isn't it OK to object to a behavior, as long as you accept the people?*
- *Isn't it important, in a democracy, to tolerate those who hold beliefs different from yours? Engage them in dialogue, not protest?*

These responses were flummoxing. Absolutely, we thought that we believed in free speech and discussion, but in this experience we wondered whose free speech is protected. The high school students who swap their pledge for entrance to college? The administrators who use their power to demand that exchange? Historically, who has been allowed "private" privacy and the right to speech? Surely not queers, whose bedrooms have been subject to scrutiny under sodomy laws and even after the repeal of such laws (Lugg, 2006). And how can sexuality, so fundamental to each of us, be rejected without also rejecting the individual? People aren't divisible from their identities, though Evangelical's administrators insist they don't reject gay people, just our "bad" queer behavior. Are the school's anti-gay statements "fighting words" that can "bring [people]…to blows"—a category of speech unprotected by the First Amendment? (Matsuda, 1993, p. 35). Or is queer-bashing so usual and expected that any words that could trigger beatings are unremarkable? Unaddressable?

The quick dismissal of Evangelical's mandatory anti-gay covenant in the "speech and belief" retorts from our colleagues was surprising, as they seemed to trivialize the hate at the core of the belief statement and ignored the collision of private (Evangelical's status as a religious educational institution) and public (Evangelical's status as an educator of teachers for public schools). In other words, these responses acknowledge a discriminatory practice but render its targets and effects—the exclusion of queer people in education—invisible. This is one of the consequences of the invasion of tolerance as the prevailing framework in play when discussing "difference" in the public sphere—in particular, in education. Tolerance leads to "category confusion" where the problem is perceived to be those "extremists" or outside agitators, not injustice (Jakobsen & Pellegrini, 2003, pp. 58–59). This framework actually functions to inhibit those vested in justice from naming the violence.

> The disabling structure of tolerance has important implications for participatory democracy because it puts those who take up political activism in any form at risk for charges of extremism. (Jakobsen & Pellegrini, 2003, p. 59)

Tolerance translates as an inability to differentiate between claims, because active tolerance supports "both sides of an issue." Through this tolerance framing, perpetrators of hate get neatly obscured, and audiences are asked not to acknowledge and notice hate but to "tolerate both sides of a conflict" (Jakobsen & Pellegrini, 2003, p. 59). In this way, the state—which once sanctioned race-based redlining and required race-based restrictive covenants to control and curtail the movement of people of color in the United States, social policies (not just individual acts) that have shaped the landscape of our communities—now supports lavender-lining by allowing institutions to exclude queers from education places under the rubric of tradition (Evangelical appealed to tolerance, for example, when they claimed that their practice of screening out LGBTQ students was just a form of "traditional Christianity").

So, what should we do when free speech is linked to private belief in this somewhat convoluted way—religious teacher education programs can ask their students to demonstrate convictions that are counter to public mandates of nondiscrimination and can then go on to prepare those students to teach in public schools that will require adherence to those same mandates of nondiscrimination (at least on paper)? Or, when public schools, under the guise of "choice" and "discipline," outsource public schooling to the military, and when criticisms are raised, state that the military is simply one among many options in a marketplace of schools? In these framings, those who critique religious teacher education regulations requiring that students pledge support for discrimination are *antireligion*, while those who critique the incursion of the military into public education are *anti-choice*. In both contexts, when questions such as ours are raised about the appropriateness of links between religious and military institutions to public education, the pushback is that we are shutting down free speech, inhibiting the military from its right to access the public sphere, and encroaching on the right of people and organizations to believe that homosexuals are "wrong."

As sex-positive feminists aware of the polarities and debates characterizing the feminist "sex wars" of the 1980s (Duggan & Hunter, 2006)—that pornography is not speech, but woman-and-child-damaging action, and should not be protected; that the first to be censored and criminalized under porn-suppressing laws would be (and were) queers and our publications—we tread gingerly in this realm. We are opposed to censorship of any sort. Yet.

When HOME—shame-baiting men organized as the problematically named *Heterosexuals Organizing for a Moral Environment*—comes each semester to the campus at Northeastern Illinois University (where Erica teaches) and distributes wildly homo-hating literature about queers, the administration, when asked to respond by the school's LGBTQ students, says it can do nothing because the university is a public institution and HOME has the right to free speech.

When Tony Kushner (1998) asserts in his essay *Matthew's Passion* that "Pope John Paul II endorses murder" (¶5) through his silence about the beating, torture, and death of Matthew Shepard, we want to add that Pope Benedict XVI's lack of silence is also murderous—he has claimed that queers are "intrinsically disordered" and have a tendency toward "intrinsic moral evil" (Schindler, 2005, ¶6, 7).

In a terrain of vastly unequal access to speech and to power—where silencing happens more to some than others, and when it is the threat of violence that maintains silence—we take a lesson from critical race theory, in particular the work of Mari Matsuda, a feminist scholar in the field who has noted that words can be used as weapons of assault, and that some speech should remain unspoken (National Public Radio, 2006). She points out that we support some curtailment of speech as a matter of course—libel laws, copyright infringement laws, and laws against fraud, for example—and asks "why we penalize someone who calls a doctor a quack, but we won't penalize someone who says that, by race, the doctor is inherently worthless and properly subject to extermination" (National Public Radio, 2006). Can we extend this analogy to Evangelical and ask whether teachers who have sworn that they believe homosexuality is immoral can at the same time teach that LGBTQ people are valuable, have contributed in important ways, can be loving parents, and so on? Or is their signed covenant (oath, pledge, or belief statement) *performative* speech, where "to say something is to do something beyond the act of uttering the words" (McGowan, 2002, p. 3)? Marriage vows fall into this category, as do wills that bequeath; the First Amendment does not protect these verbal actions. If they swear now that queers are immoral, are these future teachers likely to continue to manifest that devaluing belief in myriad ways in their future classrooms?

At least some research suggests that queer-condemning religious beliefs are "truths" that pre-service teachers cling to, even when they are generally inclined to include diverse content in their curricula (Huerta & Flemmer, 2005, p. 13). In particular, this appears to be the case with teachers who are deeply engaged with "total package" religions (Huerta & Flemmer, 2005, p. 3) that offer encompassing systems where truths are determinate, and life is regulated by the religion's authorities (Goffman, 1961). For example, Huerta and Flemmer (2005) report that LDS (Mormon) pre-service teachers resisted the idea of exploring content (including the civil rights movement, feminism, and queer issues) that challenged the doctrine of their religion; rather, when asked to incorporate cultural diversity into their teaching, these teachers made links to LDS histories and practices. This resulted in reading, for instance, the widespreading LDS missionary movement as an example of successful "diversity education and second language acquisition" (p. 12). Similarly, Kahn (2006) shows that teachers who are "conservative Christians" (believing in a literally, fully true Bible) have "tenacious" convictions that are incommensurable with some imperatives of culturally responsive teaching, such as affirming students' cultures and families, and developing a curriculum that reflects students' lives (pp. 363, 367). She points out that although all teachers have biases and must continually seek greater self-awareness, for conservative Christian educators this process is fraught—to fully acknowledge and celebrate the lives of their LGBTQ students and families would require either betrayal or abandonment of their religion. But the risks of certifying teachers who are unable or unwilling to accept that responsibility to their queer students are great, and the consequences for these youth are profound. Facing this crisis, teachers might respond with

Silence.

Teachers may deliberately ignore matters of sexual orientation that may surface in classroom conversations. Teachers may not react…to derogatory remarks relating to LGB persons. Teachers may deliberately omit material in their curriculum that portrays LGB persons in a positive light. Teachers may deliberately include material where LGB persons are portrayed in a negative light.… Teachers may be inclined to offer religious guidance to students…who have come out. Teachers may be inclined to out students to parents in the belief that they are helping them. (Kahn, 2006, p. 368)

Faced with these possibilities, we are inclined to rephrase the *New York Times* headlining question—"Should Professed Homosexuals Be Permitted to Teach School?"—inspired by Anita Bryant's 1970s, Miami-based, gay teacher–banning "Save Our Children" campaign (Maeroff, 1977): Should professed bigots be permitted to teach in our public schools?

Private Beliefs, Public Schools, and Queer Futures

The question is not what Evangelical should or can require of its students and faculty but what we want for and from our teachers in public schools. However, in public schools, the move to privatization complicates how speech and related issues, such as accreditation, plays out. Privatization forces us to look at what is public, once removed, or at schooling for the public but from the vantage point of a private educational institution that is accountable to narrow constituencies. For queers, this distancing is disadvantageous. We are already off the radar in any positive sense in most education spaces—schools are dangerous and threatening places for queer youth, and queer teachers are not well-protected in most school workplaces (Blount, 2005). The shift to privatized education means less unionized and more "at will" employment, and thus less-protected queer education workers, and more schools with queer-hostile administrations (Quinn, 2007). As just one more example, the increasing number of public military schools in urban centers means more schools with fewer out queer teachers, and fewer or no gay-straight alliances for students, and the depressing knowledge that expressed or known queerness is officially banned by the Department of the Defense.

But is relying on the state to regulate speech and *enforce safety* the best response to these dilemmas? We reject contemporary moves that focus only on attempts to afford rights to privacy for gays and lesbians, as these initiatives often turn on the foundations of the disavowal of rights to others, including those in non-monogamous relationships and those who are non-gender conforming. "Goodness" is a shifting, slippery ground and in any case should never be a prerequisite for participation in a democracy. Is the price of admission to a queer future *covering* or being "good gays" who avoid raising a ruckus anywhere? Instead of taking this homonormal route, instead of agreeing to paint our houses taupe, for instance, or accept exclusion, we wonder how to build the "robust pluralism" (Jakobsen & Pelligrini, 2003, p. 132) and public engagement that will make possible a changed and more just world. We think that dialogue is central to this task, but how can words push through the freighted, hateful history of oaths, statements, and covenants we've tried to outline in these pages?

Building on the maxim that the antidote to free speech is more speech, we offer a twist on fighting words—*flaunting words* that fight the censoring encroachment of privatization by staking a claim to public space and public queer futures, or counter-oaths aimed at undoing the "alchemy" of places such as Evangelical that turn students and faculty into sworn bigots. Call these vows—only not of marriage and not to a lover, but rather of solidarity to queerness, to the dream of loving widely and wildly, to an education that invites us all to enter. Our *Love Not Condemnation* pledge is one model; please send us yours.

CHAPTER 4

Troubled Gendering: Nations, Teaching Professions, and Covering

Teacher Power Button. Artwork by Unknown Artist;
Repurposed for Queer Organizing

A quote and a constellation of narratives:

> Professions are very queer things. It by no means follows that a clever man gets to
> the top or that a stupid man stays at the bottom. (Woolf, Three Guineas, 1938)

*It was 2005 and NCATE was scheduled to visit my institution. I had long aban-
doned any pretense of "dressing" in what I think would be generally perceived as
normative—which really means dressing like other women—at my job. Then, and
now, I generally wear jeans, T-shirts, and men's dress-shirts as jackets. I have a
small mustache. I wear my hair in a short mullet style through which I usually just
run my fingers before I leave my house in the morning. In my urban environment, I
believe that I do not stand out at all; I look, dare I say, like a stylish dyke. But, at
my job, where the majority of women wear suits, makeup, and styled hair—not
facial hair—I am conspicuous. As the visit approached, comments about my hair
ensued from two senior white women in charge of the visit. In public meetings they
asked, in trilling voices, who cut my hair? Several days before NCATE arrived,
one stopped me in the hallway and pointedly asked, "Do you need to borrow a*

hairbrush? I have one in my office." I declined, and retreated to my office, depressed and, despite my attempted air of flamboyance, embarrassed.

————

My own and other women's academic labor has included firming up the professional identities of men. Here's how I've seen and heard it work: An older male mentor asks his young female protégé to rewrite, revise, or edit a chapter, a paper, or an essay by a younger male professor who needs to publish, is struggling to make tenure, has trouble writing, is busy with a new family, just can't find time to get it all done. And she does. A woman who supported herself for years doing office work and now has an academic job and also many clerical skills is asked to provide those to her senior male colleague. And she does. A female graduate student sends a draft paper to her older male professor, then graduates, gets a job, and leaves town. A couple of years later she's reading a journal and there she notices her paper, published under the professor's name. She doesn't tell anyone—he's prominent in the field (no longer productive, but this doesn't seem to matter), and she is untenured. These are stories of the professional as the one-woman clean-up crew.

————

I am on a hiring committee. I ask the white male candidate if he has taken a course with the famous woman of color at his institution because her work relates to what he does. He looks away and says no. I am baffled because it seems nuts that one wouldn't take classes with her—she's the only postmodernist, the only professor who teaches queer and feminist theories, also, the only woman of color in his department. I ask a puzzled "Why?" and he stumbles through a response about bad timing and schedule conflicts. Later, he tells me privately, in what I read as a clubby-among-white-people-way, that well, of course, everyone knows she is "crazy." My gut contracts; my thoughts roil. Crazy? Knows too much? Asks hard questions? Calls out racism? Assigns queer authors? Do you mean—unprofessional—perhaps?

————

We offer these stories in an attempt to illuminate what has shaped our questions about gender and the profession. It has been our experience that it is often professional minutia that stalls work for change and justice: we are halted by bureaucracy, rules, protocol, and procedures, institutional and collegial silences around select issues, yet also by colleagues who seem eager to inform us that particular questions, actions, or requests are not approved, appropriate, or "timely." More often than not, these people who are our allies and gatekeepers in education are women; together, we are bound in by the performances of gender, whiteness, and heteronormativity that have shaped our field. The persistent "Nice White Lady" (check out YouTube for the video) teacher archetype in all its forms continues to inscribe our feminized profession and to shape our resistances. The power of this

gendered trope makes it centrally important and urgent to excavate and respond to
the real histories of activist educators. Recognizing that we reside in both places—
nice lady and resistant actor—all the time, we explore professionalism in this sec-
tion. We start with a look at the history of gender and whiteness in teaching and
investigate how this context has shaped organizing.

The Profession of Teaching, Nationalism, and Gender/Whiteness

Traditionally, professions—law, accounting, medicine—are defined in relation
to other types of employment through credential and licensing requirements
that control admittance, "status," or prestige; the relative control over work
site decision making; ability to specialize and to work in environments that
value specialization; higher compensation; and more (Ingersoll, 2007). Professions have power and professionals have autonomy (Johnson, 1972). Most
studies clearly indicate that teaching fails to qualify as a profession, as teachers
have fluctuating control over their daily working environments and are not
"well" compensated, and accreditation is regulated by external entities, including the state (Ingersoll, 2007). Feminist sociologist of education Sandra Acker
identifies that teaching has been constructed and dismissed as a semi-
profession, in particular due to its history as a feminized field (Acker, 1983).
Today, teaching continues to be a feminized and predominantly white field; in
2005, 82% of the public school teachers were female, up from 74% in 1996, and
approximately 17% were of color, compared to an overall U.S. population of
color of about 34% (United States Census Bureau, 2007; National Center for
Education Information, 2005). Like other low-paid caring work—"social work,
nursing and librarianship"—teaching is not really considered to be labor or a
profession, rather, it is what (generally) women do just because they want to
help (Acker, 1983, p. 125).

The gendering of the work of teaching, the concurrent devaluing of this
work, and the present face of the field are not accidental. The development of
universal, compulsory, free public schools across the United States was possible because of the work of women who were recruited to teach in common or
elementary schools (Martusewicz, 1994). These schools were central to nation
building, or to solidifying burgeoning U.S. ideologies: capitalism, industrial-
ism, Protestantism, and white supremacy (Wallace-Adams, 1988). In particular, white women were recruited to do the work of spreading these ideologies
through curriculum and teaching. White women were eventually permitted
access to teacher training institutions, or normal schools, as long as they were
morally fit and unmarried (Martusewicz, 1994). Acknowledging the history of
how gender, race, heteronormativity, and patriotism intersect within teaching

is instrumental to understand how and why the state regulates the profession, and to track how organizing and resistance is negotiated through the profession. Although we have previously examined regulating and anti-justice components of the profession in Chapter 3, this chapter extends this discussion and focuses on the centrality of gender to the work of teaching, and on the role of women teachers to do particular kinds of work as the *clean-up crew* for the state.

Nation building has always required control of institutional education, and white women, historically, have functioned as the cadre appointed to do the work. Scholars from a range of fields, cultural studies, education, anthropology, women's studies, and history, have documented the work of white female teachers to disseminate the ideologies of the state (Martusewicz, 1994). From Helen Harper, we borrow the term White Lady Bountiful (WLB) to describe the roles white female teachers played in empire building in Canada. Harper (2000) writes,

> The image of "Lady Bountiful" is particularly salient in terms of the teacher or colonial governess who was seen as having a unique duty to bring civilization to the "uncivilized." Initially, in the early 1800s, her role was to educate British working class women in religion, morality, and hygiene...The specific image of the white lady teacher is one of a spinster headmistress, intelligent but thwarted in her academic pursuits by her gender and possibly her social class, whose maternal instincts and academic interests have been directed towards her "Native" charges. Embodied, she was the sponge or mediating agent between subaltern and the colonial state. (pp. 131–132)

The white lady teacher is charged, implicitly, with colonizing her "native" students and molding them into good citizens of the republic.

This relationship between white women, the profession of teaching, and the aims of the state is also apparent in the United States where young, single, white women were appealed to as "republican mothers" to go west as teachers to civilize the new frontiers (Martusewicz, 1994, p. 172). Unmarried women moved into a limited role in the public sphere through their expanding roles as common school teachers. White women were recruited into teaching because they were constructed as naturally more suited to childcare, with minds less likely to be occupied by worldly issues such as economics, politics, or science, and because women were in possession of purer morals (Spring, 1996). Unstated, of course, was that women were significantly cheaper to employ than men.

The white lady bountiful teacher archetype is not the only iconic representation of "teacher" available, nor is it the case that there are no other archetypes or representations of female teachers. For example, in the United States, the black woman teacher is another noteworthy "teacher-archetype," but one with a very different history and attendant qualities from the WLB; it is shaped and inspired by such notable individuals as Mary McLeod Bethune and Sarah Mapps Douglas. These women taught in all-black schools and played leadership roles in education well before the Brown decisions, and in their communities and the broader society (Lerner, 1992). We have focused on the WLB because of the contemporary linkages between the regulatory powers of professionalisms and gender and the persistence of white, "straight" women in the profession. Shifting the foundational concept of the teacher—such as by drawing on archetypes other than the lady, and by highlighting teachers and educators whose work, identities, and definitions of teaching expose the sexual and racial contracts in education—is one possibility that may allow us to reveal and challenge gendered and racialized norms that are embedded in the profession.

Teaching is not the only semi-profession where white women have been used to execute a gendered, racialized, and class-based surveillance. Social work was also historically a field where women gained access to the public sphere and employment for ideological reasons; it too offers feminized work that is intimately linked to the economy and to the political needs of the nation-state. In particular, social work has played a role in shaping identities to meet the demands of new modes of production. Notably, the industrialist Henry Ford was at the forefront of social work when he sent investigators into workers' homes to regulate "morality," which, for Ford, meant monogamous heterosexuality—married couples were preferred; unmarried ones sent to court to marry—and Christianity, all in the name of industrial productivity (Martin, 1994). Female social workers and teachers were viewed as cheap, malleable, and relatively unthreatening decoys, and as the "clean-up crew" for white supremacy, capitalism, and imperialist expansion. Nice ladies, but still enforcers.

Although there is some dialogue about whiteness and femininity in the field of teacher education, we are skeptical about how successfully these works have infiltrated teacher education programs or professional development initiatives in North America. Despite the gendered field, our informal surveys suggest that there are almost no mandatory gender and education classes in teacher education programs, and feminist analysis and theory are often erased or marginalized from multicultural social foundations classes in pre-service programs.

Strategies of mobilization and resistance must be also located in this history of the feminized field. White women who participated in early progressive educational reform initiatives used gender, and more specifically maternalism, heteronormativity, and patriotism, to access leveragability in the public sphere. As feminist historians who research women teachers have noted, these middle-class white women reformers considered the "interests of the family and community as central to the state" and used the construct of "municipal house-keeping" (Rousmaniere, 1999, p. 153), casting themselves as the housekeepers, to access public voice. In Chicago, like in many other urban contexts across the United States, women played a central role in creating social welfare policies: Their status as patriotic women was seen as affording them unique expertise and access to dedicate to the advancement of families, thus, they were considered integral to state improvement. Although these progressive era strategies—starting kindergartens, offering cooking and sewing lessons for girls, advocating for laws to protect children and women—did achieve important successes, they often used constructs of white maternalism to animate heteropatriotism, or patriotism made fungible with perceptions and practices of heterosexuality. White women's political work was, therefore, trivialized or, as in Chicago, attributed to gender stereotypes, not to socialist commitments, feminist organizing, and labor activism.

> Like the traditional view that women taught school because they loved children and not for money, some supporters of the federation saw [Irish American teacher and unionist Margaret] Haley's group as self-sacrificing angels for civic reform. The Archdiocese of Chicago described the teachers' victory as a moral one and not one of self-interested teachers or suffragists. (Rousmaniere, 1999, p. 157)

White women (and to a lesser extent bourgeois black women) used their social and political position as mothers to advocate for social welfare programs for "lesser" but still "worthy" women, such as the poor, un-partnered mothers, widows, and so on, a strategy that has resulted in longer-term political and social costs, including the reinforcement of a racialized and gendered nation-state (Hancock, 2004).

Stereotypes about which kinds of women and mothers are "unfit," "lazy," and "unworthy" have long been used to develop a national common sense, a collective understanding that informs our thinking about human capacity and worth (Winfield, 2007). This, in turn, has both fostered and been used to justify violent, genocidal, and eugenicist policies that continue to frame how women can and do participate in the public sphere. Select white and heterosexual women, framed as actual or potential "respectable" mothers, and their "worthy" offspring are prioritized as de facto "good families" that can mobilize both public sentiment and reshape public policies. Bodies that do not fit—undocumented, black, disabled, queer, or non-gender conforming—do not command the same empathy or political capital and they are often viewed as unfit parents, "at risk" youth, or not-children-but-adults when being adjudicated, or simply as not quite fully human.

For example, when Elvira Arellano, the undocumented mother of a documented child, Saul, refused deportation and stayed for a year in a church in

Chicago, motherhood did not afford her political privileges. Instead, a mainstream-right backlash developed against immigrant mothers who give birth in the United States to documented children, termed "incubators" or women who come to the United States to give birth to "anchor babies" (Hooten & Henriquez, 2006, ¶3). When the Public Broadcasting Service (PBS) children's TV show *Postcards to Buster* visited two "wholesome"—country-living, dairy-farming, civil-unioned—lesbian moms in Vermont and their three kids, U.S. Education Secretary Margaret Spellings critiqued the show and PBS (according to Concerned Women for America, PBS is constantly advancing a pro-pansexual agenda—if only!), and affiliates pulled the episode (Boehlert, 2005). African American women and families continue to be disproportionately negatively affected by the child welfare system and the prison industrial complex, and by assumptions that African American families, specifically those headed by women, are less capable (Roberts, 2003). When data from child welfare agencies is coupled with justice data, the bias against black mothers is stark. The state is less likely to counsel black families than white toward keeping children in the home and more likely to enter black children than white into the child welfare system (Roberts, 2003); six times more black women than white are incarcerated and many of these mothers also see their children placed in foster care or, when they are convicted of felonies, have their parental rights terminated altogether (Greenway, 2004). Women with cognitive and other disabilities, grouped together with others categorized as "socially inadequate classes," including "Feebleminded...Diseased...Blind... Deaf... Deformed" (Laughlin, quoted in Winfield, 2007, p. 86), were among the first targeted for "mandatory sterilization" by eugenicists throughout the early twentieth century; by 1930, these laws were on the books in 30 states (Winfield, 2007). Disabled women continue to be affected by this history; today they are still frequently denied the right to be sexual and to parent (Garland-Thomson, 2002). First Nation women across North America continue to lack adequate reproductive rights, a condition linked to violent histories of forced sterilizations of Native women and forced removals of their children to boarding schools (Smith, 2005). Conversely, the spectacle of the pregnant transman in 2008 (protected by his legitimate heterosexual marriage and his relatively gender-conforming identity) has incited only seemingly limitless voyeurs, not investigations of parental fitness by social workers (Trebay, 2008).

Other feminized fields, such as nursing, where labor organizing has been vibrant in recent years, have recognized that the gender and race stereotypes that have been associated with the work and the concurrent feminization of the field need to be publicly addressed and challenged. For example, in 1999 the nurses union in England decided to ceremonially banish Florence Nightingale because she was perceived as antithetical to the future of the profession of nursing. Despite her "real" history as a medical anthropologist, a statistician, and an inventor, she was thought to telegraph the wrong image for the future of nursing—"the lady with the lamp" who is "white and well to do" and "subservient to doctors and tyrannical to her staff" (Brindle, 1999, ¶1).

> Wendy Wheeler, a nurse and health visitor from the union's London health committee, said the profession had to start to "exorcise the myth" of Nightingale. Her legacy, or its interpretation, had held nursing back too long. "What is clear is that the British establishment sought from the very origins of modern nursing to sanitise nursing and ensure that its heroine would be acceptable: a white, English, middle class, Protestant woman," she said. (Brindle, 1999, ¶5 & ¶7)

As the U.K. nurses union recognized, gendered and racialized public images and histories of do-gooders need to be challenged if the semi-profession of nursing is to flourish and change. This kind of public challenge is seemingly invisible in education. Rather, with a dogged monotony, Hollywood circulates repetitive iterations of white lady bountiful—tousled blonde Michelle Pfeiffer saving "at risk" students (read, urban youths of color) by taking them out for expensive dinners in the Hollywood film *Dangerous Minds* (1995) or the eerily similar earnest and willing to sacrifice it all Hilary Swank in *Freedom Writers* (2006)—with little critical reaction from teacher unions.

Perhaps in response to the proliferation of these white savior-lady images, what is clear to us after a few years on the "social justice" and "critical" educational conference circuit is that no decent left or progressive educator seems to want to be perceived as teaching or organizing like a girl, which must evoke for some throwing like a girl—all limp-wristed wind-up and no sure aim—you know, something really embarrassing. Of course, with the WLB lurking, it's easy to worry about being confused with the all-sacrificing teachers in *Dangerous Minds* and *Freedom Writers*, or about being mistaken as one of those fresh-faced Teach for America missionaries—recruited at only the best Ivy League universities and exclusive liberal arts colleges—who, with a few week's "training," are sent off to the colonies...oops, excuse us...schools, to spend a few years saving poor people. In these versions, teaching is the gendered province of the mockable duped, the naïve, and the do-gooder, and not an arena of social ferment and where radical change movements are populated by tough, informed, and pointedly political women. Unfortunately, critical pedagogy, to which many politicized educators look when seeking a community in the field, also seems burdened with a gendered archetype, which we could call the "last authentic dude" or LAD for short. The LAD takes up more space in education's social imaginary than is good for our health. It's also important to note that the LAD is not a counter to the WLB; they are both debilitating forms. As a corrective, we suggest that teaching and organizing like a girl or a woman could, and we think should, evoke the rebellious histories of outspoken activist teachers—from Ellen Gates Starr and Margaret Haley on through to Septima Clark, Mary Church Terrell, and others. Teaching like a riot girl or teaching like a riot, girl! that *is* critical pedagogy.

The endurance of the nice white lady icon in teaching dampens more than our memories of activist teacher histories and our appreciation for teaching like a girl; it inhibits certain people from entering the field because their lives, bodies, and politics have already been scrubbed from the profession. Where are the flamey queer men? The crips? The radical black feminist activists? The out diesel dykes? The ex-cons, high school dropouts, first-second-fourth-time-college-failures? The tattooed, the hair-dyed, and the pierced? In teaching, the nice white lady we imagine acting firmly, but with a smile, patrols teacher education classrooms for signs of waywardness. For example, any man interested in elementary education is still rendered suspect, as Acker wrote in 1983. "Men who wish to teach such [young] children run the risk of being branded as sexually deviant" (Acker, 1983, p. 134).

We offer this abbreviated history of the WLB and teaching because it informs how we understand our own work within a feminized profession. In education, professional norms are too often the subtext for our disqualification, and these racialized and gendered standards are actively interrelated with state ideologies. As we've shown, being a good mother is available only to select few women, and being a good professional teacher is embedded in this same history. Being a good teacher, just as being a "fit mother," is intimately imbricated in the practice, and the desire to unquestioningly do the work of the state—*to be the one-woman clean-up crew.* To not ask too many questions. To sit tight and hold still for patriarchy, white supremacy, and other inhumanities. Although no one is (now or yet) calling us unfit mothers, the detractions from the work for social justice chronicled in this book include accusations that we are not qualified, not professional educators or real scholars, and that we are divisive. We challenged these assessments but nevertheless, as we've noted, bore the brunt of these accusations, which seemed both gendered and regulatory, in and through a field dominated by women. Good women and nice lady teachers are produced, not simply through racist state policies and discriminatory practices, but through inducements to professional norms and both subtle and overt requests to cover our differences.

Professionalism as Covering

Within the gendered landscape of education, our work persistently raises questions about how the profession participates in regulating boundaries between what issues are appropriate for professional concern, and what are private matters. The conference we attended at Evangelical (Chapter 3) was of a public organization dealing with the issues of preparing teachers for public education, and the mandate to "teach all children" is commonly accepted in the field. But, as outlined in previous chapters, sexual minority youth and families are rejected as part of what constitutes the public in education. Sexual identity is seen as a private choice or identity, a lifestyle problem, and not as a public concern. When raising issues related to LGBTQ lives—political issues that we considered not just appropriate for our profession, but also central to the goals of creating a just society—our colleagues frequently responded as if we were showing "our privates" in public.

Our experiences with the profession, related to our attempts to change policies and practices, moved us to ask, specifically, what it means to be a professional or even a *semi-professional*. The definition of the term is self-referential. A professional is someone who acts like how a member of the profession *should*. Although the term, professional, generally incorporates public behaviors and attitudes, it is also defined in relation to the private or personal, and, largely, by what professionalism is not.

Professionalism is not wearing a hoodie, baggy pants or too-short shorts. It is not using a toothpick in public. It is not divulging *too much* about your private life. It is not professional to get a tattoo of your lover's name on your neck, yet it *is* professional to wear jewelry on your hand that signifies you are having sex, and to talk about and show pictures of your engagement, your wedding, and your honeymoon (during which everyone knows you—*wink, wink*—supposedly had lots of sex with your new husband or wife). Professionalism is aftershave lotion...worn by men, and shaved legs...on women. It is showing up "on time." It is writing in a particular genre and style, and honoring canons, traditions, and conventions, "just because." In short, professionalism is largely a kind of cultural capital available to a narrow few, and also a malleable term used to disqualify those perceived to not fit in the profession. The consequences are steep. Being designated unprofessional can be a cover for termination. Angela Davis was fired from her position as a professor of philosophy at the University of California at Los Angles (UCLA) in the spring of 1971 for supporting the Soledad brothers. The University of California stated that Davis's "advocacy constituted 'unprofessional conduct'" (Aptheker, 2006, p. 241). Women school superintendents in the mid-21st century were frequently terminated because they were labeled unprofessional. The evidence of unprofessionalism included absences from their jobs (because of mandatory unpaid maternity leave) and lower academic credentials (due to lack of access to higher education) (Blount, 1998).

In the field of education, we observe that professionalism has a colloquial meaning that is mostly about decorum represented through the body and its adornments, clothing, hairstyle, and actions and how we are "getting along" with others; in our field and practice, it is gauged also through complaints— "She didn't behave professionally: she wore biker shorts, had a piercing, included a nude in her teaching portfolio, let her tattoos show"—that we've heard about student teachers. What can be professed "professionally" is what has already been accepted or mandated by the field, but in education, where there is no commonly understood knowledge base, the field guards its boundaries in other ways, such as by scrutinizing "styles" of professionalism.

As we have experienced, when these disciplinary and professional allegiances are troubled, the troubler may have her credibility questioned and be sanctioned or ejected. However, those who deviate or leave pose a problem for those that remain and adhere. Stacey (1999), in her analysis of the fragile boundaries between the social science disciplines (specifically Anthropology and Sociology), writes about disciplinary organization being as anachronistic as "19th century political maps" and yet the anachronistic academic organization possesses power (p. 695). Disciplinary practices shape not merely our collective and individual "professional identity," but also our ways of reading and knowing, and our understanding of what we can and should do with the tools we acquire through our education.

> Disciplines actually do discipline their members by structuring our access to particular discursive communities. Disciplinary institutions establish the journals we are expected to receive, if not read, the professional organizations we are expected to join, the meetings we attend, the curriculum we teach and learn, the peer reviewers who evaluate our work, and even the consequential quotidian geography of our social networks and contacts. (Stacey, 1999, p. 693)

What if our allegiances are shaped, through the disciplinary and professionalizing process, narrowly to this "quotidian" geography, and not to justice? Larger attacks on civil rights are visible in our disciplines and professions, just as they are visible in our lives and communities outside the university. Just as regulatory representations of "unfit" mothers resonate through society to create collective understandings of human value, and these shared ideas support policies that shape lives, the dominant representations of a neutral and obedient "professional" shut down possibilities for more dynamic work in our various fields. Instead, too aware of the ways that the toxicity of isolation, reprobation, and disqualification are quickly attached to women's work and lives when they deviate, many claim a comfortable and uncontested identification with *professional*. Many of us, including teachers and professors of education, "cover" (Yoshino, 2006a).

Covering, as Yoshino (2006), building on Goffman, notes, is different from *passing*. Passing requires one to actively fake or pretend to be something she is not, while covering requires that one simply cloak, appropriately, in the normative mantles of the profession. Yoshino traces recent court cases, where the courts support "protection" for minorities, but not the behaviors associated with those groups, highlighting what is clearly the false distinction between belief or action and the bodies attached to these beliefs and actions.

> In such cases, the courts routinely distinguish between immutable and mutable traits, between being a member of a legally protected group and behavior associated with that group. Under this rule, African-Americans cannot be fired for their skin color, but they could be fired for wearing cornrows. Potential jurors cannot be struck for their ethnicity but can be struck for speaking (or even for admitting proficiency in) a foreign language. Women cannot be discharged for having two X chromosomes but can be penalized (in some jurisdictions) for becoming mothers. Although the weaker protections for sexual orientation mean gays can sometimes be fired for their status alone, they will be much more vulnerable if they are perceived to "flaunt" their sexuality. Jews cannot be separated from the military for being Jewish but can be discharged for wearing yarmulkes. (Yoshino, 2006b, ¶17)

This distinction is salient for us, because the body is always attached to its act, but it is only an act—whether throwing a kiss or wearing a kippah—that *flaunts* a status.

Demands for *covering* are the most recent manifestation of how our profession polices its boundaries and works as a conservatizing force. As in our Evangelical trip, it is OK to be gay as long as you do not ask for rights, name or point out policies that are hateful, or look or act in ways that make others feel uncomfortable. The less than lukewarm framework of multiculturalism, which does not extend to include LGBTQ lives and communities anyway, makes covering possible; multiculturalism, as a theoretical framework, does not support the acquisition of rights (Jakobsen & Pellegrini, 2003). *Fairness rather than justice, tolerance but not rights, personal responsibility instead of community or collective accountability, except when "market driven"*—this neoliberal terrain discursively works to disqualify many. If you get along with the rest of us (which means acting and looking like the rest of us) and do not ask for those damn rights (which for you, we will term *special rights*), then you are OK. And tolerance should not be our goal, as noted previously (Chapter 3). "Tolerance is certainly an improvement over hate, but it is not the same thing as freedom" (Jakobsen & Pellegrini, 2003, p. 45). Tolerance takes the focus off the hateful and violent structures and systems and locates the problem (intolerance) and remedy (change your attitude) among individuals (Jakobsen & Pellegrini, 2003, p. 52).

This is a distinct turn from the civil rights gains against the systemic and whole group-excluding discrimination of previous decades. Yoshino (2006b) argues that a "subtler form of discrimination has risen...[that] does not aim at groups as a whole...[but] at a subset of the group that refuses to cover, that is, to assimilate to dominant norms" or, in other words, that dares "to be openly different" (pp. 34, 35). In Yoshino's analysis, today some "good gays" can access state recognition—civil unionize (maybe even marry!), adopt, keep their jobs—if they perform appropriately, homonormatively. Similarly, recent work in queer theory that locates sexuality in practices of citizenship, statehood, and nationalism points to the demand for assimilation as a retraction of rights and, more importantly, as an acquiescence to deeply problematic constructions of the state (Agathangelou, Bassichis, & Spira, 2008; Puar, 2007; Duggan, 2003).

> The collaboration between heteronormativity and patriotism allows for certain forms of queerness (or sexual "deviance") to be incorporated into the project of national reproduction while others are rendered continually abject, unworthy or unable to be assimilated into either hetero—or homonormative citizenship. (Agathangelou et al., 2008, p. 127)

Following this logic, if you support the military, are prepared to "cover" and pass as if you do, or engage in marriage, home ownership, two-parent families, monogamy, and massive consumption, and in other "coverings" of difference or indicators of alignment with normative ways of living, you are worthy of incorporation into the state and might be eligible even for some social protections. If not? Oh, well, too bad—your family forms, living arrangements, and more will now be disparaged and framed as unworthy of support.

Frustrated by the constraints of professionalism, we elect to "study up." In her article *Up the Anthropologist*, Laura Nader (1972) reminds anthropologists of the importance of "studying up." She notes that researchers are conditioned to "study down" or to examine those with less power and privilege: children, prisoners, poor people, and so on. Yet, Nader writes, it is increasingly important for anthropologists to study up by focusing on "the colonizers rather than the colonized, the culture of power rather than the culture of powerlessness" (Nader, 1972, p. 289). As academics, it is easier to study down than up. But, this produces asymmetrical scholarship; for example, academic disciplines become well informed about the lives of the poor, but under-informed about, for example, how the lives of the wealthy require the lives of the poor. Nader's challenge is epistemic and political. What we research—the fundamental unit of analysis—matters.

This book applies "studying up" to the field of teacher education. How does the profession actively work to hinder and restrict prospective teachers' deepening knowledge about culture and related complex and contested issues of teaching in a pluralistic and all-too-often inequitable society? What are the examples of resistance? What policy recommendations can we offer? The following chapter offers a concrete manifestation of "studying up."

CHAPTER 5

Studying Up: Policy Activism

Accredit LOVE Not Condemnation T Shirt Design.
Artwork by Jenay Gordon

In 2005, while engaged with the projects outlined in the previous chapters, we were lucky to encounter other Illinois queers who were working in teacher education and invested in social justice. We decided to form a group to work on social justice issues in the field, specifically those that addressed LGBTQ lives and issues. We— ultimately a fluctuating group of between four and twelve members representing ten Illinois institutions[1] of higher education—affiliated with the Illinois Safe Schools Alliance organization (originally called Coalition for Education on Sexual Orientation) and named ourselves the Pre-professional Preparation Project, or P Project. We had no funding to support our labors, but the Alliance gave us a meeting site, and we were all excited to meet each other and start working. We began by surveying all of Illinois's fifty-seven teacher education programs to assess LGBTQ course content, and faculty attitudes and self-perceived competencies related to teaching about LGBTQ lives and communities. We secured two deans of colleges of education to write a letter introducing the project and subsequently circulated this and the survey via the internet.

Despite our aggressive attempts to solicit responses, the return rate was low. After viewing the survey data, it was clear that the usual suspects—in most in-

---

[1]   Chicago State University, Concordia University, DePaul University, Illinois State University, Northeastern Illinois University, Quincy University, School of the Art Institute of Chicago, University of Chicago, University of Illinois at Chicago, National-Louis University.

stances, queer friends and colleagues—participated. Almost all the responses indicated a belief that pre-service teacher preparation programs must include LGBTQ
people, and most of the faculty surveyed stated that they did work to address
LGBTQ issues. The majority of the responses came from the Chicago-based institutions. But, despite the narrowness of the sample, additional findings and contex-
tual interpretations of these results were telling. Although those who responded were
interested in and committed to including LGBTQ materials in their courses and
received support from colleagues and administration to do so, they did not feel at
all adequately prepared or competent. Many identified that the resources they used
were outdated or old, and LGBTQ issues often came into pre-service programs in
the form of the iconic tragic, wounded, and potentially suicidal student. Also, the
survey specifically asked about gender identity and transgender issues, and the majority of those surveyed stated that they had no expertise in gender identity-related
topics.

    We debated what to do after these findings. The tasks seemed immense. How
do those "sympathetic" to LGBTQ issues in teacher service programs get better
resources? What to do with the sheer lack of curricular materials linked to transgendered lives? Was our survey even useful with such a low response rate? And,
how can we engage colleagues and realities outside Chicago? We decided we needed
to start—really basically—with the parameters of how LGBTQ lives and communities were visible at each of the state institutions with teacher education programs.
After much discussion, we decided to conduct a web-based "audit" of all teacher
education programs in Illinois. None can remember actually how this got started
(we were not official enough to keep minutes, which created continuity problems)
but given our experiences at Evangelical College and our knowledge of the statewide "patchwork" quilt of interest and support in LGBTQ lives, we surmised that
a review of how LGBTQ lives were present in teacher education programs, and
how institutions represented and protected LGBTQ students, staff, and faculty in
programming, policies, codes of conduct, and other ways, was an important basic
benchmark. Do teacher education programs include sexual orientation (SO) and
gender identity (GI) in definitions of diversity? Do institutions include SO or GI in
antidiscrimination language? Are there campus-wide positive LGBTQ presences,
such as those through queer clubs or offices dedicated to LGBTQ concerns, at these
institutions? Or, conversely, do many campuses stigmatize LGBTQ people by requiring pledges or oaths condemning homosexuality from students, faculty, and
staff? We wanted this to be a statewide initiative and aimed, as a result, to develop a "snapshot" of the state context for queer students generally and prospective
teachers specifically.

    In considering our project we rationalized that these would be the kinds of
questions any potential student might consider before enrolling at these institutions,

and that the web-presence of each college and university would be the first place to which students would go to find answers. We also thought that this report might be something that staff, students, and faculty employed at these institutions could later use to leverage for more inclusive curricula. Even though visible inclusion in policies and on school websites is not necessarily a guarantee that programs and institutions value LGBTQ lives—and we all know that "under the radar" work indeed happens across Illinois—in order to press for more consistent and open representation of LGBTQ issues and lives we decided that this benchmark-creating research was important and timely.

In 2007, Illinois added sexual orientation and the term "gender-related identity" to our state antidiscrimination policy (implemented in January 2008), but the survey we conducted indicated that faculty were struggling with representing gender identity in courses. This audit could let us see where and how or maybe just whether institutions were addressing the concept. Our attempts to compel NCATE to retain sexual orientation (successful) and add gender identity (unsuccessful) in the Professional Standards governing the accreditation of teacher education helped us to see that diversity and multiculturalism were not sufficient frameworks to include either SO or GI.

We trudged along, meeting every other month or so when we could convene enough people to get work done. After the initial burst of energy, and our statewide survey, some folks lost steam and our meetings, which had attracted up to a dozen people, shrank down to a consistent five or six. Off and on we talked about pausing to write grants to fund our work, in particular, to pay someone to act as a coordinator, but at the same time, we kept pushing to keep the project moving. We wrestled over what to include in the e-assessment. Harassment policies were often buried in university websites' human resources departments and difficult to find. Institutions frequently collapsed antidiscrimination policies into harassment policies. Student "codes of conduct" were often identifiable and available online, especially at residential colleges. Materials pertaining to teacher education programs were tough to locate; Illinois teacher education programs use NCATE standards and often posted their "unit" (teacher education programs) conceptual frameworks online. These always addressed diversity, which is one of the Professional Standards, and sometimes even mentioned sexual orientation though gender identity was always absent. However, course descriptions were usually minimal and syllabi were rarely posted in full. Another concern was how to weight the data. Should the presence or absence of SO and GI in campus antidiscrimination hiring policies result in the same number of points as their status in student handbooks or codes of conduct? Should we read "between the lines" and offer the same number of (or any) points to a campus Rainbow, Pride, or Prism Club as we do to an Office of Lesbian and Gay Concerns?

We searched every institution's website for the terms gay, lesbian, gen-der/gender identity, sexual orientation, queer, lifestyle, and homosex-ual/homosexuality. The variance in language across the state was fascinating; how did these institutions choose official terms for policies, and to what extent could these language choices be "read" as positions? In 2008, we were helped by the last-minute injection of labor and energy by Connie North, who had recently completed her doctoral degree and a book and was between jobs, and also by the fact-checking of Morgan Halstead, a graduate student and educator whom we promised payment (which, as of yet, we have only partially delivered). In the end, we produced a re-port card for each institution, with a grade—A through F—and an analysis of our findings.

Therese and Connie presented this work at a local social justice in education conference. While the audience was attentive and interested, many asked why we used only materials we found online. Two faculty members from one of the institu-tions we reviewed were present and insisted that we could not accurately "grade" their school based on its web presence, which they said was not well developed or tended and didn't reflect the good work they were doing in their teacher education programs. Others in the room asked, "Why look at websites at all? They just aren't that important" and "Can websites really be considered data? Is this credible re-search?" After the session, a couple of graduate students from local universities approached us to say they liked the presentation and our project and joked—sort of—that scoffing at the value of analyzing websites was a quick way to show one's age; it was something that only older, not fully web-literate individuals would do.

Finally, in the mid-fall of 2008, we were finished. We wanted to send out a flashy report to each of the institutions' presidents and the deans or chairs of their teacher education programs, post it to a website, and do a fancy press release party. We even had a promise of some funding to help with layout, printing, and web production from University Professionals of Illinois (UPI), Erica's union. We were jazzed. Then, after stalling, the union simply reneged on the support they had promised. "Potentially too controversial" is what Erica heard through the gossip chains, though we never got a direct response from union officials. Conscious that the medium is the message, and with one artist in our group reminding us of this, we struggled to find a way to make the report look good. The lover/wife of the ex-ecutive director, a tech wiz, volunteered to do the layout. Another graduate student participant proofread the materials. We sent emails encouraging each other to pull through, keep working, and show up. The only hurdle that remained was printing and mailing.

We met in late 2008, tired and slightly crabby, and all of us with the ex-pressed intent to just get the report out. After more than two years of work, we thought, "Let's just be finished with it!" We got quotes for how much it would cost *to color copy the reports for mailing to each institution and were shocked to find a range from around one to several grand. We had no money. Erica volunteered to host a money-raising house party in her basement. We contemplated whether and how we could beg or "borrow" resources from our various institutions. One faculty member volunteered to print out of his office; others suggested that we each make a few copies on our home printers.*

We were broke, but the work was done.

Visibility Matters—2008

An Assessment of Illinois Teacher Preparation Programs' Inclusion of LGBTQ Issues

Making the Invisible Visible

How visible are lesbian, gay, bisexual, transgender, queer/questioning (LGBTQ) issues in programs that prepare educators to work in schools across Illinois? Which institutions include sexual orientation and gender identity[2] in their policies? Are sexual orientation and gender identity identified in teacher education programs' conceptual frameworks? The Pre-Professional Preparation Project (P-Project)[3] seeks not only to answer these questions but also to report the results via the Visibility Matters report cards. Using only data available from university and college websites, the Visibility Matters report cards evaluate the public face of pre-professional educator preparation programs across Illinois.

Visibility Matters Methods

To evaluate the public face of the 57 pre-professional teacher education programs in Illinois, we decided to examine their websites. Although website data do not show the day-to-day activities of college campuses, they are frequently the information that is most readily available to prospective students, particularly queer students who may be reluctant to talk about LGBTQ issues with college counselors or university officials. In short, online searches offer students an anonymous way to assess whether or not a campus is a comfortable place for queer and questioning young people, has an established "out" queer community, and prepares future teachers to engage with queer students and families in their classrooms and curricula.

---

[2]   Sexual orientation—Who you are attracted to sexually, emotionally, romantically, and/or intellectually; gender identity—A person's sense or experience of belonging to a particular gender category as a woman (girl) or a man (boy), and where a person feels they fit in society's man/woman structure (Illinois Safe Schools Alliance, 2008).

[3]   The Pre-Professional Preparation Project is a coalition of faculty from colleges and universities across Illinois that prepare educators and is supported by the Illinois Safe Schools Alliance. For more information on the P-Project or the Illinois Safe Schools Alliance see www.illinoissafeschools.org.

Members of the P-Project evaluated the websites of Illinois teacher education programs from January 2007 to January 2008. Our analyses included macro level indicators such as university-wide non-discrimination policies and LGBTQ centers, offices, or student organizations, as well as education specific indicators such as sexual orientation and gender identity being included in the conceptual framework or dispositions documents from the teacher preparation program or included in course content. In March 2008, schools and programs were revisited and "graded" according to the following rubric. Importantly, during the summer of 2008, a fact checker revisited the teacher education websites to verify our point allocation and correct any errors.

Grading Rubric

Note: SO indicates sexual orientation and GI, gender identity.

90–100:	A
80–89:	B
70–79:	C
60–69:	D
Below 60:	F

University Policies (10 points)

Points are allocated if these terms are included in any non-discrimination, anti-harassment, and/or affirmative action university-wide policies.

- 5 points for SO
- 5 points for GI

Student Rights and Responsibilities (20 points)

Points are allocated if these terms are included in university-wide documents that pertain to student rights and codes of conduct.

- 10 points for SO
- 10 points for GI

College of Education (40 points)

Points are allocated if these terms are included in the conceptual framework or dispositions documents in the institutions' teacher preparation programs and/or departments.

- 20 points for SO
- 20 points for GI

Campus Life (30 points)

Points are allocated if the institution has a diversity or multicultural office that specifically addresses LGBTQ issues and/or if an LGBTQ student club exists.

- LGBTQ Office: 15 points
- Student Club: 15 points

Extra Credit (10 points)

Points are allocated if the institution mentions LGBTQ and/or gender identity issues in any teacher education curricular material found online of if the website features a notable, recent university-wide "special event" that includes LGBTQ issues.

Anti-LGBTQ (-25 points)

Points are deducted if the institution has lifestyle statements, covenants, or mission documents that actively discriminate, dehumanize, and/or marginalize LGBTQ individuals and communities.

Summary of Results

When examining the report cards, the most conspicuous finding is the overwhelming number of failing grades. 72% of the programs evaluated (41 out of the 57) received a grade of F—or a failing grade. Six programs received a D, eight a C, one a B and one, the University of Illinois at Chicago, an A. Although a few of the failing institutions (n = 4) received no points at all, the majority of the institutions received points because LGBTQ content and protections were visible in their institutions.

However, only a handful of institutions include gender identity in their antidiscrimination and student code of conduct statements. Additionally, only twenty institutions have an office that focuses on, or explicitly includes LGBTQ concerns. Of teacher education programs and departments, twenty include sexual orientation, and only one includes gender identity in their conceptual framework or their disposition statements. As this report focuses (and weights accordingly) these statements in teacher education programs, the absence of these terms specifically impacts programs' grades.

Of note is that public institutions fared slightly better than private institutions. The majority of C and D grades went to public universities. Eastern Illinois University, Western

Illinois University, Southern Illinois Carbondale and Edwardsville, Illinois State University, University of Illinois at Chicago, Springfield and Urbana all received grades above F.

We recognize that our methodology is limited and visibility cannot be gauged solely through materials available online. However, the web is an important source of information for students, and as an entry point for campus information, it is an appropriate starting point. Contact us for updates on your institution's report card (info@illinoissafe schools.org).

Recommendations, Conclusions and Future Directions

We recognize that teacher education programs across Illinois have a range of resources, and are of varying size and scope. Yet resources and size are not barriers to including sexual orientation and gender identity in policies and public statements regarding diversity. Our findings indicate that all Illinois teacher education programs and the campuses of which they are a part can significantly improve their public attention to LGBTQ issues.

Some thoughts on recommendations:

Campus Wide

- Work to ensure that campus-wide policies, e.g. nondiscrimination, harassment, are inclusive of sexual orientation and gender identity. (See Illinois Human Rights Act— 775 ILCS 5/).
- Conduct safe-zone trainings (Safe Zone Foundation at http://safezonefoundation. tripod.com/id27.html) for departments and other units across campus to educate people on sexual orientation and gender identity as well as campus climate issues affecting LGBTQ people/communities.
- Advocate with administrators to include sexual orientation and gender identity in definitions of diversity.
- Conduct a campus climate survey (http://www.thetaskforce.org/reports_and_ research/campus_climate) that assesses the campus climate for LGBTQ persons.
- Establish an LGBTQ resource center or student group on campus; ask the campus diversity center to include LGBTQ content and rights.

Education Programs

- Make visible the practices in which you are already engaging that prepare educators to be knowledgeable about and advocate for LGBTQ youth and their families.
- Ensure that sexual orientation and gender identity are included in all definitions of diversity.
- Infuse sexual orientation and gender identity topics into multicultural education and diversity courses, child and adolescent development courses, and content area specific courses, such as English and history methods courses.

- Ensure that conceptual framework and dispositions statements include sexual orientation and gender identity.
- Utilize statements from national organizations, e.g. National Council for Teacher's of English, American Educational Research Association, to advocate for the inclusion of LGBTQ topics into the teacher preparation curriculum.
- Find allies within the university as well as the community to help you advocate for changes within your teacher preparation program, e.g. students, families, and teachers from local schools, local and state LGBTQ organizations, local and state human rights organizations, teacher and faculty unions.
- Network with other educators and teacher preparation professionals. Join the Pre-Professional Preparation Project (http://www.illinoissafeschools.org/programs/public-education/)!

Authors

Stacey Horn, University of Illinois at Chicago; Kathleen McInerney, Chicago State University; Erica Meiners, Northeastern Illinois University; Connie North, University of Maryland; Therese Quinn, School of the Art Institute of Chicago; Shannon Sullivan, Illinois Safe Schools Alliance

Contributors

Melanie D'Andrelli, University of Illinois at Chicago; Ellen Crowe, Quincy University; Morgan Halstead, University of Illinois at Chicago; Pamela Konkol, Concordia University; Mark Melton, Northeastern Illinois University; Isabel Nuñez, Concordia University; Paula Ressler, Illinois State University; Kathleen Sheridan, National-Louis University; Allison Tingwall, University of Illinois at Chicago; Joy Whitman, DePaul University; Diane Zosky, Illinois State University

Comprehensive Report Card Grades	
Augustana College	F
Aurora University	F
Benedictine University	F
Blackburn College	F
Bradley University	F
Chicago State University	F
Columbia College	F
Concordia University Chicago	F
DePaul University	D
Dominican University	F

Comprehensive Report Card Grades	
Eastern Illinois University	**D**
Elmhurst College	**F**
Erikson Institute	**F**
Eureka College	**F**
Governor's State University	**F**
Greenville College	**F**
Hebrew Theological College	**F**
Illinois College	**F**
Illinois Institute of Technology	**F**
Illinois State University	**C**
Illinois Wesleyan University	**F**
Judson University	**F**
Keller Graduate School of Management of DeVry University	**F**
Kendall College	**F**
Knox College	**C**
Lake Forest College	**F**
Lewis University	**F**
Loyola University Chicago	**F**
MacMurray College	**D**
McKendree College	**D**
Millikin University	**C**
Monmouth College	**F**
National-Louis University	**F**
North Central College	**F**
North Park College	**F**
Northeastern Illinois University	**F**
Northern Illinois University	**F**
Northwestern University	**F**
Olivet Nazarene University	**F**
Principia College	**F**
Quincy University	**F**

Comprehensive Report Card Grades	
Rockford College	F
Roosevelt University	D
Saint Xavier University	F
School of the Art Institute of Chicago	B
Southern Illinois University-Carbondale	C
Southern Illinois University-Edwardsville	D
Trinity Christian College	F
Trinity International University	F
University of Chicago	C
University of Illinois at Chicago	A
University of Illinois at Springfield	C
University of Illinois at Urbana-Champaign	C
University of Saint Francis	F
Vanderbrook College of Music	F
Western Illinois University	C
Wheaton College	F

In January 2009, we mailed out a press release and sent a copy of the report to each of the schools we graded. Responses were immediate and mixed—a colleague who had attended a couple of early meetings and then stopped showing up was outraged that her school received a failing grade, because, she insisted, great things were happening that a web-analysis wouldn't catch; Rethinking Schools, the magazine for teachers, invited us to write a story about the project for publication; a colleague at one "failing grade" school told us that their dean brought the report to a faculty meeting and said that they all needed to work to improve their institution's score. Also, a local reporter for a gay paper, Windy City Times, called an institution that received a failing grade and received this curious response, which she included in her article.

> MeShelda Jackson, chair of the School of Education at Benedictine University, was eager to discuss the report with Windy City Times, but was also unable to provide any details about teacher preparation and LGBTQ issues, and did not seem entirely comfortable talking about the community: "My understanding is that they were viewing the Web site, to see how clearly we [presented] the message of different types of diversity, as with the homosexual." (Nair, 2009, ¶8)

This educator goes on to state that LGBTQ issues are "embedded within the courses... because we have to teach about diversity. And so forth. It's not a subject *we shy away from. Our instructors are keenly aware and they talk about it in the same way as they talk about a kid with a disability. That sort of thing"* (Nair, 2009, ¶8).

And, best of all, a gender justice youth activist group brought copies of the report to an organizing meeting one of us attended and announced a plan to focus their work on teacher education programs.

Trouble with *Tolerance* in Schools

Throughout this book, we have worked to highlight how the framework of multiculturalism in education does not adequately function to include LGBTQ lives and communities. Teacher accreditation entities view LGBTQ content and social justice as inflammatory and work to eradicate or minimize these topics from accreditation documents and requirements in an effort to avoid controversy. Public school officials look the other way when LGBTQ lives are raised within the context of the militarization of public education in Chicago. Evangelical College and so many similar institutions celebrate and market diversity, while the same institutions require all faculty and staff and students to sign anti-homosexual pledges. And, as our P Project Report identified, institutions and programs are wildly inconsistent when they refer to queers: terms used include alternative lifestyles, homosexuals, gay, lesbian, sexual orientation and sexual preference, and more. Gender identity and trans issues are invisible. And, when LGBTQ rights *are* asserted, in particular against cultural or religious practices that actively discriminate against LGBTQ people or equate homosexuality with pedophilia or incest, *religious intolerance, Christophobia,* and similar charges are levied against those who even attempt to highlight a failure to love or tolerate LGBTQ lives (Edwards & Kane, 2008).

We believe that queer-inclusive policies are important and urge readers to consider this kind of studying up in their state or region, but LGBTQ equity is not our only or end goal; we hope that the P Project will serve as a catalyst to all kinds of social justice–inspired investigations by teacher educators. NCATE's "Diversity Standard" won't offer much help with this. And the dustbin of educational theory and research is piled high with difference frameworks: teaching diversity, teaching so that all can learn, culturally relevant pedagogy, multiculturalism, teaching for tolerance. All of these versions often avoid queerness. They also avoid mentioning power and justice, whether or not the term "critical" is appended to them, although power and justice undergird all difference frameworks. However, difference matters when we seek parity, when we call for representation, and when we refuse stigma; it matters because justice matters. As so many have noted, justice work in education and beyond is ultimately about the redistribution of power, resources, and rights.

As an alternative to diversity frameworks in teacher education that erase queer lives and do not name power, we are inspired by Beauboeuf-Lafontant's (1999) analysis of culturally relevant teaching, which she asserts should be re-cast as "'politically relevant' teaching in order to emphasize the political, historical, social, as well as cultural, understandings that teachers bring to their profession" (p. 705). She explains that these teachers, who are imbued with what she calls "political clarity" (p. 705) and actively engaged in politically relevant teaching, are aware that "both schooling for democratic citizenship and schooling for second-class citizenship have been basic traditions in American education" (Anderson, quoted in Beauboeuf-Lafontant, 1999, p. 705). Beauboeuf-Lafontant (1999) argues that although cultural congruence between educators and students is "certainly helpful," it is "not sufficient for remedying the contemporary problems" (p. 718). Instead, the goal should be political relevancy, which is important, she claims, for three reasons that we quote at length.

> First, discussions of "culture" [including the forms of multiculturalism and diversity] as a reference for teaching can gloss over the complexity of class, gender, and ethnic diversity that exists within any "cultural" group. However, centering on the political draws attention to the active decision making and commitments of an educator to uphold certain viewpoints (e.g., hegemonic or oppositional; oppressive or democratic) that transcend culture. Second, the term "political relevance" compels us to see beyond what is sometimes presented as an essentialist quality of social groupings. The concept of political relevance maintains that there is a political history of striving to the practice of democracy in line with our founding ideals, and that this "positive struggle" has included people of *various* cultural and social backgrounds (Wills, 1996, p. 383). Last, consciously focusing our attention on the political rather than cultural experiences of students provides us with a way of productively engaging with the reality of a majority white female teaching force educating an increasingly nonwhite public school population. If we consider that the successful education of poor students and students of color hinges on *political* congruence between teachers and students, rather than on cultural similarity, we become interested in helping teachers identify and reflect on their political convictions and their pedagogy as manifestations of their stance toward the positive struggle for democracy. (Beauboeuf-Lafontant, 1999, pp. 718–719)

If taken up more broadly within teacher education, this move from cultural to political clarity (self-awareness about one's role as a political actor) could be paired with political competency (familiarity with collective histories and strategies of political action) to be parallel and interlocking goals. Together political clarity and competency as aims or even as standards in teacher education could foster more aware teachers and more activist teacher educators and, ultimately, could help preserve public education by pushing back against privatizing trends. Teachers with clearly articulated progressive political agendas and organizing strategies are emerging as a national force, creating more and easier to access radical teacher and public education activist groups across the United States and internationally, and coming together to counter debilitating changes in public education, including charter and military schools. These groups communicate online through EdLiberation, Rethinking Schools, and other lists; organize through Facebook and in the flesh; and have chapters in all major U.S. cities—Caucus of Rank and File Educators (CORE) and Teachers for Social Justice in Chicago; Teachers 4 Justice in San Francisco; La Raza Educators in Los Angeles; New York Coalition of Radical Educators (NYCORE)—and, in some instances, work together on issues of national concern through coordinated campaigns. Examples of this are demilitarized school projects recently initiated by groups in Chicago, Los Angeles, and New York and a CORE forum attended by 500 parents, teachers, students, and community members. This early 2009 event, a "state of public education" teach-in, linked Duncan's track record of school closings in Chicago to local gentrification and national policies that privilege privatizing public education (Strauss, 2009). Campaigns and events such as these, organized by radical educators and others, help to build awareness and link both issues and people; in other words, they build the political communities and competencies required to make change. And this need is urgent. For example, a focus on political competency might shift educators to address a pressing educational catastrophe: the grotesque overrepresentation of youth of color in "soft" educational disability categories in U.S. schools. Students who are poor, African American, or new immigrants acquire specific "soft" educational disabilities, such as "Mental Retardation (MR), specifically, Mild Mental Retardation (MMR), also referred to as Educable Mental Retardation; Specific Learning Disability, also referred to as Learning Disability (LD); Emotional Disturbance (ED); and Speech and Language Impairments (SLI)" (Harry & Klingner, 2005, pp. 2–3). African American students constitute approximately 17% of national total student enrollment and 33% of those labeled mentally retarded or cognitively disabled as of 2003 (Harry & Klingner, 2005). They are three to four times more likely to be identified as mentally retarded than white students and nearly twice as likely to be labeled emotionally disturbed (McDermott, Goldman, & Varenne, 2006; Reid & Knight, 2006; Blanchett, 2006).[4]

These "soft" disability practices produce and organize difference in institutionally significant ways and attach meanings to particular differences (and

[4] This disproportionality in special education has been the focus subject of two formal investigations (1982 & 2002) by the National Academy of Sciences (Harry & Klingner, 2005).

not to other differences). We make this statement carefully, fully aware that those whom the system marks as disabled are frequently the first to be targeted for the reduction of services and are already one of the most marginalized populations. But, a focus on the political competency of educators moves us, as Baker asks, to unpack educational disability discourses.

> What power relations inhere the production of categories such as normal and ab-
> normal? Are these relations worthy of perpetuation? And finally, whether in-
> tended or not, is labeling a way of morphing "disability" into the assumptions of
> an ableist normativity, with all its racial-cultural overtones, rather than question-
> ing certain privileged ontologies and epistemologies to begin with? (Baker, 2002,
> p. 689)

"Special education" categorization, we argue, perpetuates problematic assumptions about normalcy instead of disrupting them. The range of professionals and expert practices involved in this classification actually function to inhibit the recognition of the immensity of the disciplinary apparatus that is being set into motion. Through one framework these educational processes are helpful, empowering, natural, scientific, or even "just," and simultaneously these processes can track students away from education, and into *invisible* and *abnormal* identities in the blink of an eye. These discourses reify a concept of *normal*, perhaps mythic and harmful, that is layered with race, gender, sexuality, and class histories.

Educators must be able to examine these categories politically. Our discourse of educational "difference" is only a few years removed from the deprivation- or deficit-based theories that were used to justify poor educational achievements by populations that the United States classified as inferior—less than human (Baker, 2002; McDermott, Goldman, & Varenne, 2006). The origins of educational assessment in the United States are linked to eugenics and connected to practices of race, gender, and class-based tracking (Baker, 2002; McDermott, Goldman, & Varenne, 2006). In particular, gender and sexualities appear to be relatively under-theorized in special education, yet when examining the breakdown in some specific "soft" special education categories, boys are overrepresented in a number of categories—notably the behavior disordered (Harry & Klingner, 2005). Gender is not simply a factor that teachers must be able to "know," gender *structures* "soft" educational disability categories. In order to understand and to intervene in the production of youth of color as disabled, educators (ourselves included) must be able to analyze and intervene in the production of gendered norms.

What might this look like in teacher education classrooms? We suggest the need to revisit teacher education canons, and that instead of teaching about difference and offering taxonomies of how to define and engage with difference, we flip this script to teach and learn about how difference is produced, and how, as Beauboeuf-Lafontant and others note, difference is linked to power and that the ways that society notes (and marks) difference is always political. How do race, sexuality, and gender intersect and morph in tune with economic and political changes? How did the Irish become "white" (Ignatiev, 1996)? Whose knowledge is of most worth *and why* (Bruner, 1960)? And, tellingly, "who benefits" (Gramsci, as quoted in Brantlinger, 2004, p. 1)? Posing and investigating these questions potentially equips teachers with an understanding of how identity is not simply an a priori category to engage with in schools, but a system that is politically produced in institutions, including schools.

This call for politically engaged curricula in teacher education programs that challenges multiculturalism also presses scholars in teacher education to think about our work differently. In addition to reviewing curriculum, why not "study up" on our own policies and practices? Prioritizing political relevance could foster more interventionist justice-focused research such as the P Project's and that of researchers we've noted earlier. In particular, although teacher education seems to persistently cling to frameworks that do not insist on the incorporation of LGBTQ lives and communities, aiming for political clarity, competency, and relevance would demand the acknowledgment of all who seek justice.

Policy Work as Activism

Participating in the P Project also reminded us that research that highlights the failure of public policies is crucial. We continue to be shaped, politically and professionally, by policy analysis, in particular work done by antiracist feminists and others motivated by justice. The following is a small list of examples: Valerie Polakow's work documenting how welfare-to-workfare policies damage single mothers' access to higher education (Polakow, Butler, Stormer, Deprez, & Kahn, 2004); Dorothy Roberts's research on governmental child and family social service agencies that concretely names how women of color, particularly black women, are targeted as unfit mothers at every level and application of state policy (Roberts, 2003); and Ellen Brantlinger's documentation of the overrepresentation of children of color in special education (Brantlinger, 1986) and analyses of whom high-stakes testing benefits (Brantlinger, 2004). When conservatizing forces want to deny the realities of poverty and to claim that the United States is a middle-class nation, or that white supremacy and sexism are relics, or that the really important issue that educators must address is culture—think foods and festivals, here (and definitely not gender, sexuality, or disability)—collecting and circulating data that discredits these statements is threatening; it has the potential to reframe popular understandings and transform society (Lakoff, 2004).

Public policies and practices that harm communities are often maintained through the active suppression of information collection. For example, the 2003 "Racial Privacy Initiative" in California (Proposition 54), which failed to pass, aimed to prohibit the government from collecting any data about racial and gender disparity—in health, housing, employment, education, and more (Williams, 2002). As Williams noted before the vote, in an article urging voters to reject the proposition,

> In fact, the Racial Privacy Initiative is not about protecting data from being misused; instead it effectively eliminates data collection at all. If enacted, it would continue a trend begun by Ronald Reagan and pursued by every Republican administration since: limiting the accountability of public institutions by making vital public information unavailable. In such a world, there can be no easy way to know whether Native American women are being sterilized at higher rates in public hospitals than other groups. One would not be able to determine whether public schools were tracking black students into remedial classes and white students into advanced placement. Documentation of ghettoization and other patterns of residential segregation would be magically wiped from census data. (Williams, 2002, ¶5)

Although this proposition was defeated, even when this is not the formal policy of the government, "threatening" data is suppressed. In 2003, when the head of the Bureau of Justice Statistics (BJS), Lawrence A. Greenfeld, refused to omit data from a BJS report related to traffic stops and the racial profiling of the police forces across the nation, he was threatened with termination and subsequently demoted; he eventually resigned. His data demonstrated significant racial disproportionality in traffic stops (Lichtblau, 2005). Another move is to discredit entities and individuals that do collect and circulate this data. Feminist scholarship, as an example, has been derided as not credible because it is research done by "women with agendas" and thus "unprofessional," "biased," and "not scholarly" (Levine, 2002; Irvine, 2006; de Castell & Bryson, 1998). Or, funding and institutional support is withheld or not available for work that explicitly addresses gender (Association for Women in Development, 2006).[5] And, when race, gender, or sexuality is named in the most legitimate academic tomes as variables that must be taken under consideration in gauging access to healthcare, housing, employment, and education, for example, the response from those threatened by these mild requirements may be that researchers are no longer objective and perhaps even *playing the race card*, starting a *class war*, or being *angry* and *divisive*.

---

[5] In 2003, only 7.3% of U.S. foundation giving went to "women and girls" programs or initiatives (The Association of Women in Development, 2006).

Another strategy is the appropriation of justice and equity discourses in attempts to mystify or, as Lakoff (2004) would say, mislead audiences. Ballot measures, acts and laws, and other public policies are given confusing names that function to mask punitive and profoundly unequal initiatives. Recent history is littered with examples: the Defense of Marriage Act, which harms LGBTQ access to civil rights; the U.S. Patriot Act, which uses nationalism and fear to revoke fundamental civil liberties; anti-affirmative action ballot measures titled "civil rights initiatives" (in states such as Michigan, Arizona, and California), which actively withdraw civil rights from residents (for example, Proposition 209 in California in 1996 and Proposition 2 in Michigan in 2006); and G. W. Bush's 2002 Clear Skies and 2003 Healthy Forests Initiatives, which "used language that means the opposite of what it says" (Lakoff, 2004, p. 22) to gain support. Similarly, civil rights for LGBTQ people become "special rights" in anti-gay initiative campaigns from Ohio to Colorado (Greenhouse, 1998); and legislation that is organized around punitive measures (labeling, closures, and retentions) is called the No Child Left Behind Act (Lakoff, 2004; Lieberman, 2007). Organizations such as Feminists for Life, the Cato Institute, and the Heritage Foundation all appropriate equity and justice discourses in attempts to limit and curtail fundamental rights (Kumashiro, 2007). For example, the Discovery Institute, a multi-million dollar think tank, promotes antievolution teaching, curriculum, and policy in public schools with the language of critical thinking and scientific inquiry (Wilgoren, 2005). The Discovery Institute is sponsoring the Academic Freedom Act, a bill that pushes "intelligent design," or antievolution, in schools, across state legislatures. Those who oppose this bill and the establishment of February 12 (Darwin's Birthday) as "Academic Freedom Day" are labeled anti-open inquiry, and described as seeking to "stifle scientific dissent" (Luskin, 2009, ¶5). The invocation of the mantle of scientific inquiry and the term "academic freedom," used to frame the debate about evolution in schools, is a masterful and, apparently, successful strategy.

These strategies of erasure, delegitimation, and reframing permeate our highest courts and directly impact the public sphere. For example, Roberts's 2007 Supreme Court decision refused to permit voluntary racial K-12 school desegregation plans (*Parents Involved v. Seattle School Dist. No. 1*).

> "The way to stop discrimination on the basis of race is to stop discriminating on the basis of race," he said. His side of the debate, the chief justice said, was "more faithful to the heritage of Brown," the landmark 1954 decision that declared school segregation unconstitutional. "When it comes to using race to assign children to schools, history will be heard," he said. (Roberts, as quoted in Greenhouse, 2007, ¶4)

Not only does Roberts invoke the reified legacy of Brown, the pillar of civil rights in our imagined U.S. landscape (Ladson-Billings, 2004), his logic is dizzyingly circular. To erase racism, we need to be colorblind. And, of course, history is on his side. Despite scholarly work that discredits the effectiveness of colorblindness or gender-neutrality as strategies toward developing a fairer society (Winant, 2004; Williams, 1991), the myth that not-knowing will bring about not-doing persists as common sense; it is this omnipresent social mythology that allows Roberts to make his claims seem credible in the absence of any evidence.

Given this landscape, when researchers and scholars wade into these debates as active political agents, the stakes are high. In particular, around sexuality and youth, and women's health—where ideology often trumps health "facts" ("New Evidence White House Influenced," 2006)—it is vital to collect and circulate information. In particular, under the 2000–2008 federal regime of abstinence-based education, "gag-rule" abortion laws, and active targeting of LGBTQ lives (our states' ever-proliferating gay marriage, civil rights, and adoption bans), sexual health research is dangerous. In her participation in national debates surrounding sex education in the United States, Janice Irvine (2006) worries not only about how to represent the complexity of political issues, but also about how to convey the "ugly" tactics of religious groups who are avowedly against sex education in public schools and are willing to smear and sue individuals, to fabricate scholarship, research institutes, and reports, and to "bypass peer-review" (p. 491). Despite these very real threats, Irvine argues for the importance of research on "right-wing social movements" as "both an intellectual and a political project" (p. 493). Although she argues that we must meticulously counter the fabricated scholarship that regressive and punitive institutions produce, and that we must politically engage in a public sphere, she acknowledges that the conventions of academia and disciplines mitigate against producing this kind of scholarship. When women and minorities participate in politically relevant research in the public sphere, it is often dismissed as "advocacy" and not really research (p. 494).

Yet, the amount of smart work on sexuality and education grows, despite this context. For example, researchers are examining how comprehensive sex education affects contraception choices—specifically, that this education dramatically increases contraceptive use during first intercourse by young women (Mauldon & Luker, 1996). Others have found that pregnancy rates for lesbian teens are higher than for their heterosexual peers and are looking closely at these data to understand the relationship of stigma to these findings (Saewyc, Poon, Homma, & Skay, 2008). Although "abstinence-until-marriage" education has been funded at a rate of $176 million annually, studies now show, conclusively, that there is no evidence that these programs increase the rate of sexual abstinence ("Abstinence Students Still Having Sex," 2007); that a significant number of youth who participate in abstinence-pledging programs seem to attempt to keep their pledges by having only anal or oral sex, sans condoms, and were just as likely as other teens to become infected with sexually transmitted diseases (Brückner & Bearman, 2005); and that five years later, over 80% of these youth simply deny having ever made abstinence pledges (Rosenbaum, 2009).

The push to not collect data, and to refuse to name and to see policy injustices, actively reproduces a willful, systemic ignorance. This argument is made by Sedgwick in her work on heteronormativity and HIV policy, where she argues that particular ignorances "correspond to particular knowledges and circulate as regimes of truth" (Sedgwick, 2003, p. 9). Ignorances can be cultivated, produced, and actively maintained, and they can also be challenged. Given this context, we argue that policy research—like all research—can count as a kind of activism, when performed in and for the public sphere. Whether named or not, research is always for something and against something else, and this inherent though often unstated positioning shapes how questions are framed, what is prioritized, and more. Facts never speak for themselves. Rather, we should claim the opportunity to name which research (policy, law, and so on) is moving toward social justice and the creation of a more democratic, humane, generous society, and which is not.

In our next and final chapter, we consider how some emotions—in particular, anger and shame—are used to regulate the borders between the public and the private, and how they work to silence queers. We argue that these feelings are legitimate responses to institutions and a political state that systemically deny many their rights, and, further, that exploring feelings is an important aspect of participatory research. Finally, we explore the potential of flaunting feelings as a strategy for organizers.

CONCLUSION

Volatile Affect: Resisting Shame and Stigma in the Profession

We started this work, in part, because we believed that as educators we were required to be accountable to our publics for our professorial positions. Holding our professional associations up to higher standards appeared to be a part of our job descriptions. And, as queers with deep investments in the movement toward social justice, advocating for public policies that supported queers to flourish in schools seemed like a responsible and *just* professional action. If—with all of our relative power and privileges—*we* cannot stand up and publicly support what we perceive to be the "right thing," how can we go into schools and expect teachers, parents, and students to do this work? How can we expect queer youth to be out and to fight white supremacy or homophobia? Yet, despite our sense of righteousness, the more than two-year-long "professional" series of projects recounted here has often left us with mild political professional depression—we have had bad feelings.

Clearly, we did some things "wrong" in each campaign or, more generously, could have made different choices. For example, we did not always secure many direct public allies for our projects, and this affected our ability to move the work along. In one instance, we collaboratively created an organization, Teachers Against Militarized Education (TAME), but as a working unit of two people, we found ourselves trying to "do it all": the time needed to invite others to join the group was in competition with the time we needed to make a fact sheet and to organize a public forum about the issue, and so on. This reduced our ability to catalyze resistance to military schools in Chicago.

Our frequent state of duo soloness (with the exception of the work on the P Project) can be explained, in part, because we did not have any easy means to mobilize our colleagues. Both of us have experience organizing outside of the profession, but less inside. To an extent, we have each cultivated and appreciated an outsider stance in the field of education. While we felt like outsiders, at times, because of professional conventions (as we've discussed previously), doing the networking that campaign-building requires is time-consuming, sometimes difficult to accomplish, and often diminishes in priority when other, more urgent work must be done. However, these were not the only reasons why we had so few professional collaborators. Many colleagues expressed admiration for what we were doing but frequently would not participate. They wanted to hear about the issues, sympathized with us, and wanted to write about the political or theoretical components of these projects—but they didn't want to take on the profession, show up in person, or add their names to a letter. Many others were "crazy busy right now." Some folks were worried about tenure and job stability; this reaction seemed reasonable, and also sad. Others simply did not want to do the work. Often they were uneasy about confrontation. *Couldn't we just make our points more* professionally—*and* politely? *Couldn't we be a little less strident? Couldn't we get someone with just a little more credibility on our side? Did we have to be so public about it all? Wasn't there another way?* As we analyzed these responses, we thought it's possible that we are simply "unattractive" individuals who were unable to garner support for these important projects because of our personal failings or poor professional skills, but in the end, we find this hard to believe. A more likely explanation is that the work we were doing threatened an important professional status quo and, therefore, stigmatized us and—by association—all who worked with us.

In previous organizing, often outside the profession of education, we have gained strength from our collaborators, from their bodies on the ground with us. We offered credibility to each other by valuing the passionate labor we brought to our tasks and not through claims of special expertise or academic degrees. But the instances we recount here were somewhat different. Often, more of our aligned colleagues were online and not a physical presence. In addition to the associates who didn't want to or could not be involved, the queers we could see sometimes didn't seem to want to see or be seen with us. And this brings us back around to our *bad* feelings: As often as we were energized by what we believed was the *rightness* of this work, we also felt agitated and depressed by the isolating conditions of the labor. We felt like bad people, marked by this aloneness.

Our experiences at Evangelical and with AERA also evoked a host of other emotions: embarrassment ("unprofessional"), fear ("we are first contacting you"), and shame ("reckless and inappropriate behavior"). The anger and love that inspired our actions and was referenced in materials we distributed was dismissed, while the potentially crushing anger of the large and powerful institutions, AERA and Evangelical, registered as the righteous responses of betrayed institutions, as exemplified by the horrified reactions of some of our colleagues and administrators upon hearing about our intervention at the conference.

Feelings are not simply by-products of organizing or research, they are, as we have attempted to chart throughout this work, a central component of contemporary political life. As Feel Tank Chicago points out, politics is a "world of orchestrated feeling" (2008, ¶3). It is instructive not only to name emotions and to explore how they regulate participation in everyday civic life (who are we afraid of and why?) but also to explore how feelings shape our engagement with our professional and academic lives. For example, when accused of being unprofessional in a number of contexts, we felt embarrassed and paralyzed, except for a fleeting but panicky urge to prove we *were* professional. Aiming at "emotional epistemology" (Feel Tank Chicago, 2008, ¶2), or knowing through (attending to) feelings in this way—thinking of them contextually as meaningful in social ways—has been a useful focus of our participatory research because these feelings demonstrate how affect is used to regulate not just our field's definitions of professional and scholarly activities, but many institutions as well.

The (attempted) production of feelings to regulate and to secure state-sanctioned goals is not new—panic, terror, and shame are central to the stories of redlining and white flight, lynching and genocidal policies of child removal, and eugenics—and is central to the neoliberal agenda. The fear of terrorist violence in your neighborhood, of illegal aliens taking your job, of welfare freeloaders and prisoners using your hard-earned dollars, of the "worst of the worst" deviant sex offender teaching your children, the feelings of disgust, fear, and anger produced through the public repetition of these tropes, all help to justify expanding the punitive arm of the state and cutting any social services. The circulations of these feelings become "affective economies" that "seduce us all into the folds of the state" (Agathangelou, Bassichis, & Spira, 2008, p. 122). While neoliberalism shifts our understanding of what is public and what is private, the accompanying production of feelings of disgust, anger, and fear have been harnessed expertly by the right. More directly, these fears fuel support for the surveillance of those public spaces and institutions perceived as inhabited by the working poor. For example, the fear of bad and unruly black and brown children is used to fuel the privatizing choice movement in education. These fears are produced also as threats—to marriage, safety, and traditions, which require *defense*: Department of Defense public schools, a Defense of Marriage Act, the U.S. Patriot Act, and on and on. Our professional associations participate in these "affective economies" by producing feelings, too—for example, by granting approval and inclusion to those who act professionally and by threatening to censure and shun those who are unprofessional. Just as nationalism, patriotism, and other state-normativities are maintained through practices and affects, so too are professionalism's norms.

This chapter also explores how public feelings function to regulate life for queers. Specifically, the work of noticing and naming the queer body is also about identifying affect; making heteronormativity or queerness visible in educational spaces incites a range of emotional responses: disgust, hostility, outrage, and charges of being "inappropriate" (de Castell & Bryson, 1998). All these feelings are important places for analysis and inquiry. We want to better understand the role of our anger in particular as feminist philosopher Jaggar terms it, an "outlaw emotion":

> Outlaw emotions are distinguished by their incompatibility with the dominant perceptions and values…. Outlaw emotions stand in a dialectical relation to critical social theory: at least some are necessary to developing a critical perspective on the world, but they also presuppose at least the beginning of such a perspective. (Jaggar, 1989, pp. 144–145)

Outlaw emotions can provide important insights into structural inequities. Jaggar argues that oppressed people have a kind of "epistemic privilege" and their responses "are more likely to be appropriate than the emotional responses of the dominant class. That is, they are more likely to incorporate reliable appraisals of situations" (Jaggar, 1989, p. 146). Yet, as Cvetkovich (2003) points out, women and people of color have less credibility than those with power when they report trauma and their feelings about it. Professional organizations and institutions get to be legitimately angry at our "unprofessional" behavior; our anger is erased and attributed to the bias of our bodies. Their anger is apt; ours is inappropriate. In fact, our anger is seen as another manifestation of our failure as professionals and as a confirmation of our wrongness, our stigma.

Goffman defines stigma as an "attribute that is deeply discrediting" and that reduces the bearer "from a whole and usual person to a tainted, discounted one" (Goffman, 1963, p. 3). Stigma requires a political context with power differentials. While both of us have job security, employment, and full identities outside of our profession, the power of a profession to create norms (and de facto deviants) is immense. These norms silence because the corollary of stigma is shame. In the profession of education, as in other fields, we argue that covering (as discussed in Chapter 4) is mandated not only through the unspoken and spoken norms and "dispositions" circulating around the profession, but also through shame. Our varied experiences clearly highlight the work of stigma and shame—*our own feelings when raising our hands or standing up to ask if LGBTQ issues are included in the definition of diversity, being the source of uncomfortable "jokes" about fashion and hairstyles, standing awkwardly around when people are discussing weddings and engagements, being refused eye contact by the fey men and the butchy ladies at professional meetings when queer issues are not raised, being told we are detracting from race issues when naming homophobia, weighing whether you should out yourself in deeply heteronormative spaces, having to care for other peoples' feelings.*

While anger is a legitimate response to institutions that systemically deny the right to participate or that propagate hate, it can be dangerous to show that emotion in public spaces. We also heed Lorde's warning that displays of "outlaw emotions" will be used against those who are marginalized. As Lorde writes in her essay, "Uses of Anger,"

Everything can be used / Except what is wasteful / (you will need to remember this when you are accused of destruction) (Lorde, 1984, p. 127)

Anger can be a vital tool to mobilize communities and individuals for change, yet it is simultaneously an emotion that is too frequently used as a reason to devalue or erase the responses or analysis of those who are marginalized. And shame results, in part, from an inability to express anger. Shame always has two aspects, "painful individuation" and "uncontrollable relationality" (Sedgwick, 2003, p. 37); shame isolates and yet requires a social environment, and the ground of connection is the body. Through the lens of queer theory, the experience of shame can be seen as useful—it highlights bodies, behaviors, meanings, affects, and cultures that are non-normative and might otherwise be overlooked (Gay Shame, 2007). At Evangelical, our public queerness made it harder for the hoping-to-be-invisible queers in the room to stay unacknowledged; the woman who trailed us to the bathroom seemed equally compelled and revolted, drawn to us and ashamed of our connection. Shaming is what is happening when the cadet is called "faggot" (his peers are the unnoted audience).

Shame also works to maintain social and institutional silences. The possibility of shame is what keeps professionals in line (our colleagues judge our "fit" to the profession). In fact, in professional contexts, we negotiate shame every day, in particular when working to advocate for, or even to make visible, those targeted by the state for destruction and surveillance. An exploration of shame can serve as another model of the value of charting and analyzing feelings and affect, as it allows us to describe the power of the profession to normalize and to repress dialogue and change. Tracking shame and attempts at shaming and the corresponding volatile affects—silence, anger, sadness—offers a map of anxieties that are not only personal but also professional. Throughout our organizing in education we have been reminded that to be a professional is to be silent—to cover—at least about some things, and that those who are not silent should be ashamed.

Lorde (1984) notes, "it is not…anger…that will destroy us, but our refusals to…learn within it" (p. 130). Heeding and expanding on her warning, understanding feelings as produced and as productive (when studied) has been an important analytic strategy for our participatory research. In particular, it helps us reframe shame—ours and others'—as a political and privatizing tool and marks it as something that happens in public and yet is corrosive to the public. An insight from disability studies is useful here: Linton (1998) points out that disability theorizing is not intended to offer "a parable for the forgotten and downtrodden," it is rather a "problematizing agent" that points to the need for something different (p. 185). Similarly, our focus on feelings in research is useful not because it may encourage a sympathetic response from readers. Instead, we contend that focusing on feelings can help us see and challenge norms, including of professions and institutions that claim dispassion even as they produce feelings to achieve oppressive ends. Feelings indicate openings, if we are paying attention. In this way, feelings can be *tactic-triggers*.

In this book and in our on-the-ground labors, we reject the privatizing and even the personalizing of feelings as indicative of the normalizing demands endemic to education. Emotions regulate power relationships within the profession and within the state, and we argue that our feelings are pedagogical, pervasive, and public, rather than private and local. In fact, these feelings should be flaunted.

Flaunting It: A Strategy

How do we finish this book, when our work is still in process? Both of us are suspicious of the kind of endings that promise radical salvation in *10 Easy Steps*. Social justice essays and books, including many of our own, often suggest that more coalition building, more meetings, and more dialogue will lead to redemptive change. It is temping to offer that kind of prescription here, because, well…organizing matters. Community matters. Dialogue matters. Even in the absence of tidy concluding thoughts, focused work done with others is important: it offers the pleasurable experience of acting in tandem, even when the goal of justice remains elusive.

To return to the example of our intervention at the teacher education conference at Evangelical College, we were not at all sure that wearing our handmade queer-love positive T-shirts or inviting everyone to sign a *Love Not Condemnation* Pledge would result in a change of future conference locations. But the tees and love oaths, as both art and activism, countered Evangelical's largely secret hate oath campaign against gays and lesbians. They let us flaunt our opposition and this made us happy, which is important—feeling good is what will sustain the work ahead. Movement building and sustaining is about *acting* and *feeling* for justice. We invite you, our colleagues and allies, to use this anti-covering, even stigma-cherishing, strategy—*flaunting it*—as a way to push back at constraints placed on us in public spaces, including education.

Crucial to the Evangelical experience and to *flaunting it* is keeping the issues, struggles, and feelings—even angry love—public. Change, we are convinced, happens only when a robust and engaged populace participates in a public sphere. In this book, we have argued that our profession *must* change, that it must be remade from the inside out and from the outside in. We have no template for that remaking, yet we know that we have strong histories of public resistances to draw from: San Francisco's 1966 transgender-initiated Compton cafeteria riot against the harassment of trans folks and sex workers; the millions of Latinos and others who marched in the streets across the United States on May Day in 2006 to protest the criminalization of those who are undocumented and to push back for amnesty for all; the leadership of the men incarcerated in Walpole prison who, in 1973, tired of systemic racialized abuse from the guards, seized control of the prison, asked community members to come inside and observe, and fought to have their work protected and recognized with a labor union; Mamie Till's defiant decision in 1955 to have an open casket public funeral for her teen-aged son, Emmett, who was killed by white supremacists; the public struggles to remove homosexuality as a form of mental illness from the 1974 *Diagnostic Statistics Manual* (Stryker, 2008; Parker, 2004; "Thousands March," 2008; Bissonnette, 2008; Psutka, 2008). These, and many other examples, demonstrate that this work of building and sustaining an "audacious democracy" must be collective and must be done in public (West, 1997).

Claiming this history as our foundation, this book chronicles some present consequences of the neoliberal retreat from the public, including privatopias and boutique schools, and points toward the possibility of others, such as the militarization of everyday life, expanded disenfranchisement, increased deportations and more heavily fortified borders, multiplying police forces and prisons, and explicit, cradle-to-grave life plans for the "best and brightest" and everyone else. *Flaunting* has several implications that recommend it as a strategy of opposition to increased privatization. In addition to always remaining public and thus invitational, and with the portent of participation, this work is tactical, and always improvisatory and emergent—it takes form from the issues and feelings of the moment. And, *flaunting* connotes creativity and flair; it's performative. As shorthand, we could say it's anti-lesson plan, pro-parade, pro-open enrollment, and very queer.

Starting Where We Are:
Changing Institutions and Ourselves

For those with at least one foot in a university, starting where we are means making a persistent alliance between theory and our intellectual work, and activism—an imperative we argue is urgent now. We must challenge what counts as an *appropriate* scholarly endeavor and, as Laura Nader proposed in 1969, "study up" on the culture of power. We must question and change the "commonsense" educational practices that disempower and under-educate so many (Kumashiro, 2004). But, changing institutions requires doing the difficult work to understand our "cop-in-the-head" and our "cop in the heart," or how institutions and their corresponding regulatory practices live in and through each of us (Boal, 1990; Rojas, 2007). This imperative to internal decolonization is difficult to fully comprehend, much less achieve. We have each asked ourselves these questions: When have I not acted or spoken because I didn't think I was smart enough? Am I waiting for a leader to step up and take charge? Am I overlooking opportunities to live and love more robustly, because I fear disapproval? For all of these questions, and so many more, we push ourselves to understand what orthodoxies we live inside, and how these constrain not only our individual possibilities but also social change.

We need not just to write and profess and think about what the world we want to live in could be, we need also to think, act, and craft that world into being, starting with ourselves as we work with others. To paraphrase the words of the prison abolition organization Critical Resistance, *to dismantle oppressive institutions we must change the way we live and think and relate and then build new organizations from the inside out and outside in, together* (Critical Resistance 10 Publications Collective, 2008). The time won't ever be better and the stakes will always be high. So do something *in community*; start anywhere; start now, don't wait.

In this book, we have argued that our profession is deeply and historically flawed, and that public education in the United States has always aimed to sort and sift youth, to create populations that are disposable, superfluous, and designated for low-wage employment. It continues to be a battle to challenge this reality as it persists and takes new forms—from the residential schooling movement, to selective enrollment and charter schools—and to expose and intervene in how race, gender, class, sexuality, nationality, ability, and more matter, desperately, in the culling of our children and communities. What happens in public schools is linked to the economy; what happens in classrooms is shaped by housing and healthcare. In other words, the problem with the pedagogy in public schools isn't really that it's not critical enough, or that teachers can't or won't do their jobs well—it's that all that is public, including schools, is under attack.

We have also described strategies we've tried and problems we've encountered in our attempts to craft solutions to these issues. Convinced that a complete rethinking and reworking of the field is necessary, we turn to you. Our primary recommendation is to begin. To be of use, as the poet Marge Piercy (1982) writes, when "the work of the world is common as mud," consists, in large part, of showing up and following through (p. 106) and, sometimes, knowing when to get out of the way. Decide when, where, how, and with which allies and tactics to tackle the tasks ahead. But whatever you do, flaunt it.

Below we share some scenarios we are trying; these are aimed at building not just new organizations but also new selves and societies from the inside out and the outside in. When you invent your own and have invited others to join with you (because, as we've noted, one and even two is a pretty lonely movement), document everything you do. Post the images. Write a book. Illustrate a series of comix. Virally populate cyberspace with the news. Propose a manifesto based on your work. Make a movie about it and upload it to YouTube. And email us—Therese at tquinn@saic.edu and Erica at e-meiners@neiu.edu.

So, from the inside out,

- Become an active member of your professional association and ask queerly justice-seeking questions.
- Join a reading group with staff and students—undergraduates—at your university.
- Select a non-canonical book to use in your teacher education class. How about Angela Davis's (2003) radical policy analysis *Are Prisons Obsolete?* Or Alison Bechdel's (2006) graphic memoir, *Fun Home?* Or, the artfully disruptive *The Interventionists: Users' Manual for the Creative Disruption of Everyday Life* by MASS MoCA (2004)?
- Start organizations such as TAME, Teachers Against Militarized Education, to raise the visibility of social issues educators should engage with.
- Write a platform manifesto, rant, and get others to offer feedback and to sign on, and work to translate it into institutional policies.

From the outside in,

- Work with artists, parents, youth, community-based organizations, ad hoc neighborhood groups, and other allies to change your profession.
- Lose the expert hat and be a worker in movements addressing issues that affect education, such as housing, healthcare, and public transit.
- Bring art and beauty and feelings to professional sites—jettison any lingering political depression and instead ask about…you decide.
- Have parties at your house and invite all the justice thinkers and workers you know, feed them, and ask them for $5 to support a project.
- Organize a public event—at the Jane Addams Hull-House Museum in Chicago, Free Soup Tuesdays draw a crowd to eat and talk together about current issues.

Your labors for social change will not be without precedent and should never be lonely; rather, the best part of working for justice in the broadest sense is that it overflows with connections to the vital past and possibilities for our present and futures-in-the-making. There are powerful examples to draw on; look to radical, social justice-oriented, lady teachers and their sissy colleagues for inspiration, in addition to the activists noted throughout this book.

For us, flaunting is a tactic that *feels right. Flaunting it* means speaking back when queer (or other justice) issues are dismissed as too confrontational for public dialogues, and too trivial for public institutions. *Flaunting it* means organizing against Department of Defense schools because their policies construct youth of color as both inherently disciplinarily deficient and in need of a military masculinity that requires homophobia and misogyny. *Flaunting it* means naming the ways our profession professes ignorance and attempts to silence justice while it actively colludes with policies and practices that do harm to youth and communities. *Flaunting it* means naming the cowardice of resource-laden professional organizations that so often fail to live up to their missions to serve the public good. *Flaunting it* calls for archiving the past/present/future evidence of our activism and the work of our sister activists in education, against disappearance and planned memory losses. *Flaunting it* means doing meticulously crafted collaborative policy research that names injustice and inequity. *Flaunting it* responds to the dilemmas we've outlined here—the privatization of the public sphere; the privatization of public policies; and professionalism as silence/silencing—by insisting that our riots of publicly expressed joy and anger are powerful tools of resistance and change. So, flaunt it.

On the Pleasures of Activism

In the dark times, will there also be singing?
Yes, there will be singing.
About the dark times.

—Bertolt Brecht

What characterizes Brecht's poem above is a kind of lovely and joyous insistence that something can and will be done in the face of injustice. One recognizes this same obstinate spirit throughout Therese and Erica's book.

The resistance to oppression is what makes this world habitable for all of us. Although it may sound straightforward, we must take our vocation as human beings very seriously. Making an effort to be human and to make the world more humane is a job demanding twenty-four hours a day. And although this work is hard and can even infuriate us at times, it must always be pleasurable as well. Activism that does not inventively engage our sentient *and* sensual selves and does not give us joy or make us happy is unsustainable and also unattractive. As Emma Goldman famously quipped, "If I can't dance I don't want to be in your revolution."

In addition to enjoying the process of transforming the world, our activism should include friends, family, co-workers, and lovers as well as give us the opportunity to befriend strangers. Making the world more just is not something that should be discrete or separate from our "normal" working lives and identities, or something that we do in privacy. The notion of a secret, essential, personhood that enters into and then is able to retreat out of a political, public sphere has been debunked over and over again. As an ideological construct, the artificial insistence on the division between our public and private lives does not contribute to a participatory democracy but is instead heavily invested in a public that exists only to police the private, all the while asserting that people are "free" to do as they like as long as they keep it to themselves. The personal is political, and collective action and conviviality interrupts the "techniques of isolation" (which Michel Foucault describes in *History of Sexuality*) that identify and set apart some individuals as perverse, different, or abnormal. We should all take pleasure in "flaunting" our activism with style, and with as many people as possible!

When I first became the director of the Jane Addams Hull-House Museum, I would often find myself lingering over letters that the reformers from the Progressive Era wrote to family and friends describing long bike rides along Lakeshore Drive on sultry evenings that ended in beer gardens or jumping spontaneously into Lake Michigan for a cooling swim. It is hard to imagine

Jane Addams and her cohorts having fun or at play. Because they seem so serious and formidable, it is easy to forget the pleasure they took in sharing a delicious meal in the Residents' Dining Hall, or the delight they had in singing songs, reading poems, or laughing hard at each other's jokes. They were people who spent their entire lives working for the common good, transforming the nation with their efforts, whether it was establishing the nation's first juvenile justice court, traveling to the Hague to discuss world peace, fighting for immigrant rights, closing down sweatshops, or struggling for fair housing and public health. It is the right to the simple pleasures in life for all people, regardless of race, class, gender, or sexual orientation, for which Jane Addams and others fought so hard.

Taking pleasure in life and the struggle for justice is what I believe sustained the Hull-House reformers over the forty years that Addams lived and worked in Chicago. As part of the first generation of college-educated white women in the United States, the Hull-House reformers blurred the lines between their private lives and public efforts. They politicized the domestic economy and turned the prevailing division of public and private on its head. The collective living conditions at Hull-House Settlement included apartments, public kitchens, and communal dining halls that allowed the reformers to read to one another in bed and to talk over dinner about legislation they were working on. This does not mean they were always working, quite the contrary. Their efforts, for example, to pass the Factory and Workshop Bill in 1913, which laid the groundwork for the eight-hour workday, were as much about stopping the oppressive sweatshop and factory owners from taking advantage of working people as it was about the gentle insistence on the need to stop work and to have fun. The refusal to schizophrenically separate their desiring, political selves and everything they cared so deeply about from other intimate parts of their daily lives contributed to the creation of a richly textured public space at Hull-House that was engaging, challenging, and supportive.

Whether it is through song or dance, writing protest letters, or speaking out at large public forums, Therese and Erica's book also reminds us that the public sphere has always been a space of contestation and a site that needs to be creatively imagined and re-imagined. In order for a participatory democracy to flourish, we must encourage public forms of expression that give voice to dissent. It is no accident that Therese is an art educator and that both she and Erica are creative activists. Artists have so often played an important role in the creation of the public sphere. In a world with so much un-making, whether it is due to war, or the destruction we have so selfishly engaged in on earth and in its environment, the role of artists and those who make, imagine, and represent the world with a new vision is absolutely essential. This art of making is full of risk and peril because it tangibly challenges power and visibly provides an alternative to the way things are by allowing us to see how things might be.

Many people are surprised to find out that Jane Addams, who most of us know as America's first woman to win the Nobel Peace Prize, was also considered at one point in history to be "Public Enemy #1" and also "The Most Dangerous Person in the United States." Addams was considered "dangerous" because she was a suffragist who agitated for equal rights for women and an unwavering peace activist in a time of war. But the crucial reason why she was under FBI surveillance was for the simple reason that she opened the Hull-House Settlement doors, where she lived and worked, to people who did not always have popular or mainstream views. Addams created opportunities for people to assemble and discuss controversial ideas, argue, and grapple with hard issues. The Hull-House Settlement was the place where social reformers, scientists, artists, and others were able to unleash their imaginations and envision a different world. This commitment to radically democratic and inclusive public space challenged power and authority and made some people consider her "dangerous."

The other often unspoken reason why Jane Addams was considered so "dangerous" was that she unabashedly chose Mary Rozet Smith as her closest confidant and partner. The hushed debates that erupt into public uproars now and again about whether Jane Addams "was or wasn't" lesbian reflect legitimate intellectual interest in the cultural evolution of language and the history of sexuality but more often than not are a manifestation of homophobia expressed as a pathological anxiety about our historical icons and what is appropriate and acceptable. Addams lived in a long-term, committed, primary relationship with Mary Rozet Smith. They owned property together in Hulls Cove in Maine. When they traveled together, they traveled as husbands and wives did: sharing the same room and bed. Addams addressed Smith as "dearest." She used phrases such as "I am yours 'til death," a phrase that is unambiguously joined in U.S. culture to the vows of marriage. During one separation, in describing how much she missed Smith, Addams wrote, "There is reason in the habit of married folks keeping together." Their relationship to each other was recognized by their close associates and intimates as being unique, like no other relationship that the two had. "Jane Addams was gay," as one friend of mine has said, "like the day is long." Yet, the struggle to accept her as a gay woman continues and may be longer than we anticipate.

Although some might dismiss this debate as passé, sensationalist, or unimportant in relation to all the other important issues we should be addressing today in our fight for justice, I disagree. We too often suffer from selective his-

torical amnesia. Looking back to our activist forefathers and foremothers, con-
necting our struggles with theirs, and remembering the pleasure they took in
making a more just society are an important part of the continuous remaking
of the world. Recognizing this continuity reminds us, as Ella Baker was fond of
saying, that "the struggle is eternal. The tribe increases. Somebody else carries
on."

Lisa Yun Lee, Director, Jane Addams Hull-House Museum,
University of Illinois at Chicago

REFERENCES

AAA opposes U.S. military's Human Terrain System Project. (n.d.). Retrieved February 2, 2009, from http://www.aaanet.org/issues/AAA-Opposes-Human-Terrain-System-Project.cfm

Abstinence students still having sex: Study tracked 2,057 young people in government-funded programs. (2007, April 16). *Associated Press.* Retrieved January 8, 2009, from http://www.msnbc.msn.com/id/18093769/

Acker, S. (1983). Women and teaching: A semi-detached sociology of a semi-profession. In S. Walker & L. Barton (Eds.), *Gender, class, and education* (pp. 123–139). Barcombe, UK: Falmer Press.

Agathangelou, A.M., Bassichis, D. & Spira, T. (2008, Winter). Intimate investments: Homonormativity, global lockdown, and seductions of empire. *Radical History Review, 100,* 120–143.

Alvarez, L. (2007, February 14). Army giving more waivers in recruiting. *The New York Times.* Retrieved September 21, 2008, from http://www.nytimes.com/2007/02/14/us/14military.html?_r=1&scp=1&sq=military%20recruitment&st=cse&oref=slogin

American Bar Association (ABA). (n.d.). *ABA policy on legislative and national issues.* Retrieved July 12, 2008, from http://www.abanet.org/policy/GreenBookChp13.pdf

American Educational Research Association (AERA). (2007, January). Key AERA policy documents on position taking and policymaking and on social justice. *Educational Researcher, 36*(1), 49–54.

American Library Association (ALA). (2007, December 4). *Press release: ALA President Loriene Roy responds to attempts to remove "The Golden Compasss" from library shelves.* Retrieved July 16, 2008, from http://www.ala.org/Template.cfm?Section=News&template=/ContentManagement/ContentDisplay.cfm&ContentID=169110

American Psychological Association (APA). (2007, August 19). Reaffirmation of the American Psychological Association position against torture and other cruel, inhuman, or degrading treatment or punishment and its application to individuals defined in the United States code as "enemy combatants." Retrieved February 2, 2009, from http://www.apa.org/governance/resolutions/councilres0807.html

Anchors Away (2007, January). Monthly newsletter. *Save Senn Coalition, 2*(5), 1–2.

Anderson, E. (2006). *Out of the closet and into the courts: Legal opportunity structure and gay rights litigation.* Ann Arbor, MI: University of Michigan Press.

Andrews, K. (2002, March). Movement-countermovement dynamics and the emergence of new institutions: The case of "white flight" schools in Mississippi. *Social Forces, 80*(3), 911–936.

Anti-gay measure has apparently failed. (2000, November 11). *USA Today.* Retrieved February 8, 2007, from http://www.usatoday.com/news/vote2000/or/gay.htm

Aptheker, B. (2006). *Intimate politics: How I grew up red, fought for free speech, and became a feminist rebel.* Emeryville, CA: Seal Press.

Area 26 & JROTC Fact Sheet (2007, October 15). *Programs.* Retrieved January 10, 2008, from http://www.chicagojrotc.com/fact_sheet.jsp?rn=9040770

Arenson, K. (1997, November 8). Furor over a sex conference stirs SUNY's quiet New Paltz campus. *The New York Times.* Retrieved July 15, 2008, from http://query.nytimes.com/gst/fullpage.html?res=9B01E4DB1539F93BA35752C1A961958260

Asimov, N. (2008, June 27). S.F. school board kills PE credit for JROTC. *San Francisco Chronicle,* B1. Retrieved July 8, 2008, from http://www.sfgate.com/cgi-bin/article.cgi?f=/c/a/2008/06/27/BAJ411FPOE.DTL

Association for Women in Development (2006). Where is the money for women's rights? Assessing the resources and the role of donors in the promotion of women's rights and the support of women's rights organizations. Retrieved December 20, 2009, from http://www.awid.org/go.php?pg=where_is_money

Baker, B. (2002). The hunt for disability: The new eugenics and the normalization of school children. *Teachers College Record, 104*(4), 663–703.

Baker, E. (2007, January). From the desk of the president. *Educational Researcher, 36*(1), 37–38.

Banchero, S. (2007, October 15). Chicago military schools: Reading, writing, recruiting. *Chicago Tribune,* 1,1.

Bartlett, L. & Lutz, C. (1998). Disciplining social difference: Some cultural politics of military training in public high schools. *The Urban Review, 30*(2), 119–136.

Beauboeuf-Lafontant, T. (1999, Summer). A movement against and beyond boundaries: "Politically relevant teaching" among African American teachers. *Teachers College Record, 100*(4), 702–723.

Bechdel, A. (2006). *Fun home: A family tragicomic.* New York: Houghton Mifflin.

Begos, K. (2002). Against their will: North Carolina's sterilization program. *Winston-Salem Journal.* Retrieved May 5, 2008, from http://against theirwill.journalnow.com/

Belluck, P. & Zezima, K. (2008, July 16). A 1913 law dies to better serve gay marriages. *The New York Times.* Retrieved September 24, 2008, from http://www.nytimes.com/2008/07/16/us/16gay.html?_r=1&sq=gay%20 marriage%20boston%20economy&st=cse&adxnnl=1&oref=slogin&scp= 2&adxnnlx=1222264987-dj+npTrOm+pIYvcKUEPpQQ

Bissonette, J. (2008). *When the prisoners ran Walpole: A true story in the movement for prison abolition.* Boston, MA: South End Press.

Blackmar, E. (2005). Appropriating the "Commons": The tragedy of property rights discourse. In S. Low & N. Smith (Eds.), *The politics of public space* (pp. 49–80). New York: Routledge.

Blanchett, W. J. (2006). Disproportionate representation of African American students in special education: Acknowledging the role of white privilege and racism. *Educational Researcher, 35*(6), 24–28.

Blount, J. (1998). *Destined to rule the schools: Women and the superintendency 1873–1995.* Albany, NY: State University of New York Press.

Blount, J. (2005). *Fit to teach: Same-sex desire, gender, and school work in the twentieth century.* Albany, NY: State University of New York Press.

Blume, H. (2008, June 12). School rallies around dismissed Watts teacher. *Los Angeles Times.* Retrieved February 4, 2009, from http://articles.latimes. com/2008/jun/12/local/me-jordan12

Boal, A. (1990). The cop in the head: Three hypotheses. *The Drama Review, 34*(3), 35–42.

Board to vote on more inclusive gay high school plan. (2008, November 18). *The Huffington Post.* Retrieved December 11, 2008, from http:// www. huffingtonpost.com/2008/11/18/board-to-vote-on-more-inc_n_ 144763.html

Bob Jones University tells gay alumni: Don't come back. (1998, October 24). *Amarillo Globe.* Retrieved June 9, 2008, from http://www.amarillo.com/ stories/ 102498/new_bjuniv.shtml

Boehlert, E. (2005, February 4). Paralyzed broadcasting system. *Salon.* Retrieved January 10, 2008, from http://dir.salon.com/story/news/feature/ 2005/02/04/pbs_and_conservatives/index.html

Bohrman, R. & Murakawa, N. (2005). Remaking big government: Immigration and crime control in the United States. In J. Sudbury (Ed.), *Global lockdown: Gender, race, and the rise of the prison industrial complex* (pp. 109–126). New York: Routledge.

Borda, O. (2001). Participatory (action) research in social theory: Origins and challenges. In P. Reason & H. Bradbury (Eds.), *Handbook of action research* (pp. 27–37). London: Sage.

Bousquet, M. (2008). *How the university works: Higher education and the low-wage nation.* New York: New York University Press.

Bousquet, M. (Undated). Foreword. *Workplace: The Journal of Academic Labor.* Retrieved December 25, 2008, from http://www.cust.educ.ubc.ca/workplace/issue7p2/index.html

Brantlinger, E. (1986). Making decisions about special education: Do low-income parents have the information they need? *Journal of Learning Disabilities, 20,* 95–101.

Brantlinger, E. (2004, February). An application of Gramsci's "who benefits?" to high-stakes testing. *Workplace: A Journal for Academic Labor, 6*(1). Retrieved January 8, 2009, from http://www.cust.educ.ubc.ca/workplace/issue6p1/brantlinger.html

Brindle, D. (1999, April 27). Nurses snuff Nightingale image: Union votes to ditch "outdated" lady with the lamp model. *The Guardian.* Retrieved July 10, 2008, from http://www.guardian.co.uk/uk/1999/apr/27/davidbrindle

Browne, K. (2007, May). Military sex scandals from tailhook to the present: The cure can be worse than the disease. *Duke Journal of Gender Law & Policy, 14,* 749–790.

Brückner, H. & Bearman, P. (2005, April). After the promise: The STD consequences of adolescent virginity pledges. *Journal of Adolescent Health, 36*(4), 271–278.

Bruner, J. (1960). *The process of education.* Cambridge, MA: Harvard University Press.

Bureau of Justice Statistics. (2000, July). *Sexual assault of young children as reported to law enforcement: Victim, incident, and offender characteristics,* 6. Retrieved May 20, 2008, from www.ojp.usdoj.gov/bjs/pub/pdf/saycrle.pdf

Bush welfare plan promotes marriage and work. (February 27, 2002). *CNN.* Retrieved April 22, 2007, from http://archives.cnn.com/2002/ALLPOLITICS/02/26/welfare.reform/index.html

Butin, D. (2007, Summer). Dark times indeed: NCATE, social justice, and the marginalization of multicultural foundations. *Journal of Educational Controversy, 2*(2). Retrieved September 21, 2008, from http://www.wce.wwu.edu/Resources/CEP/eJournal/v002n002/a003.shtml

Cantu, C. (2008, January 29). Testimony at public meeting. Chicago, IL: Northeastern Illinois University.

Carlson, P. (2005, May 5). Taking the Bob out of Bob Jones U: Christian institution readies for the next generation. *Washington Post,* C01.

Cassidy, D. (2007). *How the Irish invented slang: The secret language of the crossroads.* Petrolia, CA: Counterpunch.

Chen, M. (2008, July/August). Home from the military. *Colorlines.* Retrieved October 10, 2008, from http://www.colorlines.com/article.php?ID=378

Chicago's largest employers. (2008). *Crain's.* Retrieved July 14, 2008, from http://www.chicagobusiness.com/cgi-bin/businessList.pl?djoPage=view_html&djoPid=1643&djoPY=@pGKJyF3ZKmUM

Cisneros, S. (1997, August 31). My purple house—color is a language and a history. *Hispanic Link.* Retrieved May 14, 2008, from http://www.gen-connection.com/English/house.html

Cohen, C. (2005). Punks, bulldaggers, and welfare queens: The radical potential of queer politics? In P. Johnson & M. Henderson (Eds.), *Black queer studies* (pp. 22–51). Durham, NC: Duke University Press.

Critical Resistance 10 Publications Collective. (2008). *Abolition now! Ten years of strategy and struggle against the prison industrial complex.* Oakland, CA: AK Press.

Cvetkovich, A. (2003). *An archive of feelings: Trauma, sexuality, and lesbian public cultures.* Durham, NC: Duke University Press.

Daley, R. (2001, Fall). Correspondence: Military academies; do teachers matter? *Education Next.* Retrieved July 29, 2006, from http://www.hoover.org/publications/ednext/3384806.html

Dangerous Minds. [Motion Picture] (1995). Rabin, S., Foster, L. & Simpson, D. (Producers) and Smith, J. & Schwab, E. (Directors). United States: Hollywood Pictures.

Davis, A. (2003). *Are prisons obsolete?* New York: Seven Stories.

Debate military training: School pupils give views at Panel in Times Hall. (1945, January 20). *The New York Times.* Retrieved September 15, 2008, from http://nytimes.com/

de Castell, S. & Bryson, M. (1998). From the ridiculous to the sublime: On finding oneself in educational research. In W. Pinar (Ed.), *Queer theory in education* (pp. 245–250). New York: Lawrence Erlbaum.

de Certeau, M. (1984). *The practice of everyday life* [Translated by Steven Rendall]. Berkeley, CA: University of California Press.

de Lauretis, T. (1991). Queer theory: Lesbian and gay sexualities. *Differences: A Journal of Feminist Cultural Studies, 3*(2), iii–xviii.

DeGeneres needles McCain on gay marriage. (2008, May 21). *USA Today.* Retrieved July 10, 2008, from http://www.usatoday.com/life/people/2008-05-21-mccain-ellen_N.htm

Demographics: Single women praise Lennar's designs, National Association of Realtors cites statistics of current homeownership. (2008, March 22). *Las Vegas Journal-Review*. Retrieved June 11, 2008, from http://www.lvrj.com/real_estate/16922561.html

Dent, D. (1996, August 4). African-Americans turning to Christian academies. *The New York Times*. Retrieved June 9, 2008, from http://query.nytimes.com/gst/fullpage.html?res=9C03E5DB103DF937A3575BC0A960958260

Dohrn, B. (2008, September 13). ARC 109 [Public Forum]. Experimental Station: Chicago, IL.

Duggan, L. (2003). *The twilight of equality: Neoliberalism, cultural politics and the attack on democracy*. Boston, MA: Beacon Press.

Duggan, L. (2004, March 15). Holy matrimony. *The Nation*. Retrieved December 10, 2006, from http://www.thenation.com/doc/20040315/duggan

Duggan, L. & Hunter, N. (2006). *Sex wars: Sexual dissent and political culture*. New York: Routledge.

Edwards, D. & Kane, M. (2008, December 24). Christophobia? Rick Warren scandal "getting weirder": Maddow. *The Raw Story*. Retrieved January 15, 2008, from http://www.rawstory.com/news/2008/Maddow_Rick_Warren_confuses_himself_with_1224.html

Eisenhart, R. W. (1975). You can't hack it little girl: A discussion of the covert psychological agenda of modern combat training. *Journal of Social Issues, 31*(4), 13–23.

Enloe, C. (2000). *Bananas, beaches and bases: Making feminist sense of international politics*. Berkeley, CA: University of California Press.

Epstein, E. (2004, February 23). Governor fears unrest unless same-sex marriages are halted, Schwarzenegger voices concern over potential civil clashes in S.F. *San Francisco Chronicle*. Retrieved December 16, 2006, from http://sfgate.com/cgi-bin/article.cgi?file=/c/a/2004/02/23/MNGJ7566RL1.DTL

Eskridge, W. (2000, November). No promo homo: The sedimentation of anti-gay discourse and the channeling effect of judicial review. *New York University Law Review, 75*, 1328–1411.

Fine, M. (1997). Witnessing whiteness. In L. Fine, L. Weis, L. Powell, & L. Wong (Eds.), *Off-white: Readings on race, power and society* (pp. 57–65). New York: Routledge.

Feel Tank Chicago. (2008). Manifesto. Retrieved November 13, 2008, from http://www.feeltankchicago.net/

Freedom writers. [Motion Picture] (2007). Devito, D., Shamberg, M. & Sher, S. (Producers), & LaGravenese, R. (Director). United States: Paramount Motion Pictures.

Garland-Thomson, R. (2002, Fall). Integrating disability, transforming feminist theory. *NWSA Journal, 14*(3), 1-32.

Gay Shame. (2007). Gay shame San Francisco. Retrieved January 8, 2007, from http://www.gayshamesf.org/

Gerber, E. (1999, July 13). George W.'s racial covenant. *Slate*. Retrieved May 13, 2008, from http://www.slate.com/id/1003204/

Gilmore, R. (2007). In the shadow of the shadow state. In INCITE! Women of Color against Violence (Eds.), *The revolution will not be funded: Beyond the non-profit prison industrial complex* (pp. 41–52). Boston, MA: South End Press.

Gladwell, M. (2008). *Outliers: The story of success*. New York: Little, Brown.

Goffman, E. (1961). *Asylums*. New York: Anchor.

Goffman, E. (1963). *Stigma: Notes on the management of spoiled identity*. New York: Prentice-Hall.

Gramsci, A. (1971). *Selections from the prison notebooks of Antonio Gramsci*, Q. Hoare & G. Nowell Smith (Eds. & Trans). London: Lawrence and Wishart.

Greenhouse, L. (2007, June 29). Justices limit the use of race in school plans for integration. *The New York Times*. Retrieved January 20, 2009, from http://www.nytimes.com/2007/06/29/washington/29scotus.html

Greenhouse, L. (1998, October 14). Justices leave intact anti-gay measure. *The New York Times*. Retrieved January 20, 2009, from http://query.ny-times.com/gst/fullpage.html?res=9D0CEED6143AF937A25753C1A96E958260&sec=&spon=&pagewanted=all

Greenway, A. (2004). When neutral policies aren't so neutral: Increasing incarceration rates and the effect of the adoption and Safe Families Act of 1997 on the parental rights of African-American women. *National Black Law Journal, 17*, 247–255.

Griffin v. School Board of St. Edward (1964). Retrieved May 20, 2008, from http://afroamhistory.about.com/library/blgriffin_v_princeedward.htm

Gunther, M. (2006). Corporate America backs gay rights: Gay rights are good business, no matter the politics. *FORTUNE Magazine*. Retrieved September 2, 2008, from http://money.cnn.com/magazines/fortune/fortune_archive/2006/12/11/8395465/index.htm

Halberstam, J. (2005). *In a queer time and place: Transgender bodies, subcultural lives*. New York: New York University Press.

Hancock, A. (2004). *The politics of disgust: The public identity of the welfare queen*. New York: New York University Press.

Harman, J. (2008, March 31). Rapists in the ranks. *Los Angeles Times*. Retrieved April 9, 2008, from http://www.latimes.com/news/opinion/commentary/la-oe-harman31mar,0,5399612.story

Harper, H. (2000). White women teaching in the North: Problematic identity on the shores of Hudson Bay. In N. Rodriguez & L. Villaverde (Eds.), *Dismantling white privilege: Pedagogy, politics, and whiteness* (pp. 127–143). New York: Peter Lang.

Harris, C. (1993). Whiteness as property. *Harvard Law Review, 106*, 1709–1791.

Harry, B. & Klingner, J. K. (2005). *Why are so many minority students in special education?: Understanding race & disability in schools*. New York: Teachers College Press.

Harvey, D. (2005). *A brief history of neoliberalism*. New York: Oxford University Press.

Heron, J. & Reason, P. (2001). The practice of co-operative inquiry: Research "with" rather than "on" people. In P. Reason & H. Bradbury (Eds.), *Handbook of action research* (pp. 144–154). London: Sage.

Herrnstein, R. & Murray, C. (1994). *The bell curve: Intelligence and class structure in American life*. New York: Free Press.

Holt, S. (2004, March 10). Workplace warms to same-sex partners. *Seattle Times,* Retrieved on February 2, 2009, from http://community.seattletimes.nwsource.com/archive/?date=20040310&slug=bizbenefits10

Hooton, A. & Henriquez, S. (2006). Immigrant rights are women's rights. *Off Our Backs*. Retrieved July 10, 2008, from http://findarticles.com/p/articles/mi_qa3693/is_200601/ai_n19511620

Horn, S. & Szalacha, L. (2007). Chicago Public Schools youth risk behavior survey, 2005. *Board of Education of the City of Chicago*. Retrieved July 16, 2007, from http://209.85.215.104/search?q=cache:IQHvB8VMhlsJ:www.oism.cps.k12.il.us/pdf/2005yrbs.pdf+2003+Youth+Risk+Survey+CDS+Chicago+Public+Schools&hl=en&ct=clnk&cd=1&gl=us

Houppert, K. (2008, April 3). Another KBR rape case. *The Nation*. Retrieved April 16, 2008, from http://www.thenation.com/doc/20080421/houppert

Huerta, G. & Flemmer, L. (2005, March). Identity, beliefs and community: LDS (Mormon) pre-service secondary teacher views about diversity. *Intercultural Education, 16*(1), 1–14.

Ignatiev, I. (1996). *How the Irish became white*. New York: Routledge.

Illinois Arts Alliance. (2005). Arts at the core: Every school, every student. Retrieved May 5, 2008, from http://www.artsalliance.org/ed_research.shtml

INCITE! Women of Color against Violence. (2007). *The revolution will not be funded: Beyond the non-profit prison industrial complex.* Cambridge, MA: South End Press.

Ingersoll, R. (2007). The status of teaching as a profession. In J. Ballantine & J. Spade (Eds.), *Schools and society* (pp.106–118). Thousand Oaks, CA: Sage.

Irvine, J. (2006). Sex lies and research. *Mobilizations: The International Quarterly Review of Social Movement Research, 11*(4), 491–494.

Jaggar, A. (1989). Love and knowledge: Emotion in feminist epistemology. In A. Garry & M. Pearsall (Eds.), *Women, knowledge and reality* (2nd edition, pp. 129–156). London: Routledge.

Jakobsen, J. & Pellegrini, A. (2003). *Love the sin: Sexual regulation and the limits of religious tolerance.* New York: New York University Press.

Jaschik, S. (2008, May 8). Michigan ruling bars domestic partner benefits. *Inside Higher Ed.* Retrieved July 8, 2008, from http://www.insidehighered.com/news/2008/05/08/benefits

Johnson, B. & Goldberg, R. (1995). Boot-camp violence: Abuse in Vietnam War-era basic training. *The Journal of Undergraduate Research, 6*(1), 7–13. Retrieved January18, 2008, from http://www.lib.utah.edu/epubs/undergrad/vol6/johnson.html

Johnson, B. & Johnson, D. (2007). An analysis of NCATE's decision to drop "Social Justice." *Journal of Educational Controversy, 2*(2). Retrieved August 10, 2008, from http://www.wce.wwu.edu/Resources/CEP/eJournal/v002n002/a004.shtml

Johnson, D., Johnson, B., Farenga, S. & Ness, D. (2005). *Trivializing teacher education: The accreditation squeeze.* New York: Rowman & Littlefield.

Johnson, T. (1972). *Professions and power.* London: Palgrave Macmillan.

Jones-Correa, M. (2000–2001). The origins and diffusion of racial restrictive covenants. *Political Science Quarterly, 115*(4), 541–568.

Kahn, M. (2006). Conservative Christian teachers: Possible consequences for lesbian, gay, and bisexual youth. *Intercultural Education, 17*(4), 359–371.

Kantor, A. & Nystuen, J. (1986). De facto redlining a geographic view. *Economic Geography, 58*(4), 309–328.

Khayatt, M. (1992). *Lesbian teachers: An invisible presence.* Albany, NY: State University of New York Press.

Koch, C. (2000). Attitudes, knowledge, and anticipated behaviors of preservice teachers of individuals with different sexual orientations. *Dissertation Abstracts International, 61*(05), 1797A. (UMI No. 9973083)

Koch, W. (2006, June 15). Development bars sex offenders. *USA Today.* Retrieved June 15, 2008, from http://www.usatoday.com/news/nation/2006-06-15-sex-offenders-barred_x.htm

Kosciw, J. G. & Diaz, E. M. (2006). *The 2005 national school climate survey: The experiences of lesbian, gay, bisexual and transgender youth in our nation's schools.* New York: GLSEN.

Kumashiro, K. (2004). *Against common sense: Teaching and learning toward social justice.* New York: Routledge.

Kumashiro, K. (2007). *The seduction of common sense: How the right has framed the debate on America's schools.* New York: Teachers College Pres.

Kushner, T. (1998). Matthew's passion. *The Nation.* Retrieved June 10, 2008, from http://web.archive.org/web/20030730084624/www.class.uidaho.edu/diversity/tkon.htm

Ladson-Billings, G. (2004). Landing on the wrong note: The price we paid for Brown. *Educational Researcher, 33*(7), 3–13.

Lakoff, G. (2004). *Don't think of an elephant: Know your values and frame the debate.* White River Junction, VT: Chelsea Green.

Lassiter, M. (2006). *The silent majority: Suburban politics in the sunbelt south.* Princeton, NJ: Princeton University Press.

Lerner, G. (1992). *Black women in white America: A documentary history.* New York: Vintage.

Levine, J. (2002). *Harmful to minors: The perils of protecting children from sex.* Minneapolis, MN: University of Minnesota Press.

Lewis, H. (2006). Participatory research and education for social change: Highlander Research and Education Center. In P. Reason & H. Bradbury (Eds.), *Handbook of action research* (pp. 262–268). London: Sage.

Li, K. (1996). The private insurance industry's tactics against suspected homosexuals: Redlining based on occupation, residence, and mental status. *American Journal of Law & Medicine, XXII*(4), 477–502.

Lichtblau, E. (2005, August 24). Profiling report leads to a demotion. *The New York Times.* Retrieved January 26, 2009, from http://www.nytimes.com/2005/08/24/politics/24profiling.html?pagewanted=print

Lieberman, B. (2007, August 9). No Child labels schools unfairly, administrators say. *Union-Tribune.* Retrieved January 17, 2009, from http://www.signonsandiego.com/news/education/20070809-9999-7m9nclb.html

Linton, S. (1998). *Claiming disability: Knowledge and identity.* New York: New York University Press.

Linville, D. (2008). Queer theory and teen sexuality: Unclear lines. In J. Anyon (Ed.), *Theory and educational research: Toward critical social explanation* (pp. 153–174). New York: Routledge.

Lipman, P. (204). High stakes education: Inequality, globalization, and urban school reform. New York: Routledge.

Lipsitz, G. (1998). *The possessive investment in whiteness: How white people profit from identity politics*. Philadelphia: Temple University Press.

Liptak, A. (2008, May 16). California Supreme Court overturns gay marriage ban. *The New York Times*. Retrieved July 10, 2008, from http://www.nytimes.com/2008/05/16/us/16marriage.html?scp=4&sq=california+gay+marriage&st=nyt

Loewen, J. (2005). *Sundown towns: A hidden dimension of American racism*. New York: The New Press.

López, I. (1996). *White by law: The legal construction of race*. New York: New York University Press.

Lorde, A. (1984). *Sister outsider: Essays and speeches*. Freedom, CA: The Crossing Press.

Low, S. (2005). How private interests take over public space: Zoning, taxes, and incorporation of gated communities. In S. Low & N. Smith (Eds.), *The politics of public space* (pp. 81–104). New York: Routledge.

Lubienski, C. (2001, August). Redefining "public" education: Charter schools, common schools, and the rhetoric of reform. *Teachers College Record, 103*(4), 634–666.

Lugg, C. (2006, January and March). Thinking about sodomy: Public schools, legal panopticons, and queers. *Educational Policy, 20*(1), 35–58.

Lugg, C. (2007, April 16). Re: Letter to NCATE. Message posted to AERA-QUEER-STUDIES-SIG@BAMA.UA.EDU.

Luskin, C. (2009, February 10). Darwin, intelligent design, and freedom of discovery on evolutionists' holy day. *US News and World Report*. Retrieved February 15, 2009, from http://www.usnews.com/articles/opinion/2009/02/10/darwin-intelligent-design-and-freedom-of-discovery-on-evolutionists-holy-day.html

Mackenzie, J. (1916, September 10). Can schools give military training? *New York Times*. Retrieved April 24, 2009, from http://query.nytimes.com/gst/abstract.html?res=9E07E1DD1F31E733A05753C1A96F9C946796D6CF

Maeroff, G. (1977, June 24). Should professed homosexuals be permitted to teach school? *The New York Times*. Retrieved September 15, 2008, from http://nytimes.com/

Marcus, R. (2005, April 11). Booting the bench: There's new ferocity in talk of firing activist judges. *Washington Post*. Retrieved October 2, 2008, from http://www.washingtonpost.com/wp-dyn/articles/A42691-2005Apr10.html

Martin, E. (1994). *Flexible bodies: The role of immunology in American culture from the days of polio to the age of AIDS*. Boston, MA: Beacon Press.

Martusewicz, R. (1994). Guardians of childhood. In W. Reynolds & R. Martusewicz (Eds.), *Inside/out: Contemporary critical perspectives in education* (pp. 168–181). New York: St. Martin's Press.

MASS MoCA. (2004). *The interventionists: Users' manual for the creative disruption of everyday life.* North Adams, MA: MASS MoCA.

Massachusetts Department of Education. (2002). 2001 youth risk behavior survey results. Retrieved October 10, 2008, from www.doe.mass.edu/cnp/hprograms/yrbs/01/results.pdf

Massey, D. & Denton, N. (1993). *American apartheid: Segregation and the making of the underclass.* Cambridge, MA: Harvard University Press.

Matsuda, M. (1993). Public response to racist speech: Considering the victim's story. In M. Matsuda, C. Lawrence III, R. Delgado & K. Crenshaw, *Words that wound: Critical race theory, assaultive speech, and the First Amendment,* (pp. 17–51). Boulder, CO: Westview Press.

Mauldon, J. & Luker, K. (1996, January–February). The effects of contraceptive education on method use at first intercourse. *Family Planning Perspectives, 28*(1), 19–41.

McDermott, R., Goldman, S. & Varenne, H. (2006). The cultural work of learning disabilities. *Educational Researcher, 35*(6), 12–17.

McGowan, M. (2002, Summer). Certain illusions about speech: Why the free-speech critique of hostile work environment harassment is wrong. *Constitutional Commentary, 19*(2), 1–42.

McKenzie, E. (2003, September 18–19). *Private gated communities in the American urban fabric: Emerging trends in their production, practices, and regulation.* Paper presented at conference on Gated Communities: Building Social Division or Safer Communities? Retrieved October 10, 2008, from www.bristol.ac.uk/sps/cnrpapersword/gated/mckenzie.pdf

McKenzie, E. (2008). Gated communities and homeowner associations. Retrieved May 20, 2008, from http://tigger.uic.edu/~mckenzie/hoa.html

McRuer, R. (2008). "Marry" me? Alternatives to Marriage Project. Retrieved September 24, 2008, from http://www.unmarried.org/marryme.html

Medina, J. (2007, September 7). Recruitment by military in schools is criticized. *The New York Times.* Retrieved October 9, 2008, from http://www.nytimes.com/2007/09/07/nyregion/07recruit.html

Nader, L. (1972). Up the anthropologist. In D. Hymes (Ed.), *Reinventing anthropology* (pp. 284–311). New York: Vintage Books.

Nader, L. (2005). *Life of the law.* Berkeley, CA: University of California Press.

Nair, Y. (2009, February 4). State colleges get failing grades on LGBTQ issues. *Windy City Times.* Retrieved February 6, 2009, from http://www.windycitymediagroup.com/images/publications/wct/2009-02-04/current.pdf

National Center for Education Information. (2005, August 18). *Profile of teachers in the U.S. 2005.* Retrieved May 15, 2008, from http://www.ncei.com/POT05PRESSREL3.htm

National Council for Accreditation of Teacher Education. (NCATE). (n.d.). Glossary. Retrieved September 19, 2006, from http://www.ncate.org/public/glossary.asp?ch=143

National Fair Housing Alliance (NFHA). (2006). *Unequal opportunity—Perpetuating housing segregation in America report.* Retrieved October 20, 2006, from http://www.nationalfairhousing.org/resources/newsArchive/resource_20628126054870386567.pdf

National Public Radio. (2006, October 26). Weighing the limits of freedom of expression. Retrieved June 9, 2008, from http://npr.org/templates/story/story.php?storyId=6249980

New evidence White House influenced FDA on Plan B. (2006, May 12). *Salon.* Retrieved February 1, 2009, from http://www.salon.com/mwt/broadsheet/2006/05/12/emergency_contraception/

Ordover, N. (2003). *American eugenics: Race, queer anatomy, and the science of nationalism.* Minneapolis, MN: University of Minnesota Press.

Oser, A. (1986, August 1). Unenforceable covenants are in many deeds. *The New York Times.* Retrieved May 13, 2008, from http://query.nytimes.com/gst/fullpage.html?res=9A0DE4DC1639F932A3575BC0A960948260&sec=&spon=&pagewanted=all

Park, P. (2001). Knowledge and participatory research. In P. Reason & H. Bradbury (Eds.), *Handbook of action research* (pp. 83–93). London: Sage.

Parker, L. (2004, March 10). Justice pursued for Emmett Till. *USA Today.* Retrieved October 6, 2008, from http://www.usatoday.com/news/nation/2004-03-10-till-usat_x.htm

Peake, L. & Kobayashi, A. (2002). Policies and practices for an antiracist geography at the millennium. *The Professional Geographer, 54,* 50–61.

Pew Hispanic Trust. (2005, June). Unauthorized migrants: Numbers and characteristics. Retrieved July 10, 2008, from http://www.pewtrusts.org/uploadedFiles/wwwpewtrustsorg/News/Press_Releases/Hispanics_in_America/PHC_immigrants_0605.pdf

Piercy, M. (1982). *Circles on the water.* New York: Alfred A. Knopf.

Pinar, W. (2006, August 22). [Review of Trivializing Teacher Education: The Accreditation Squeeze]. *Teachers College Record.* Retrieved October 10, 2008, from http://www.tcrecord.org/content.asp?contentid=12691

Plank, D. & Sykes, G. (2003). Why school choice? In D. Plank & G. Sykes (Eds.), *Choosing choice: School choice in international perspective* (pp. vii–xxii). New York, NY: Teachers College Press.

Polakow, V., Butler, S., Stormer, L. & Kahn, P. (Eds.) (2004). *Shut out: Low-income mothers and higher education in post-welfare America*. Albany, NY: State University of New York Press.

Psutka, D. (2008, June 25). Critics blast the book on mental illness. *Globe and Mail*. Retrieved October 12, 2008, from http://www.theglobeandmail.com/servlet/story/RTGAM.20080625.dsm26/BNStory/mentalhealth/

Puar, J. (2007). *Terrorist assemblages: Homonationalism in queer times*. Durham, NC: Duke University Press.

Pupovac, J. (2008, November 25). What happened to Pride Campus? *Chicago Journal*. Retrieved December 11, 2008, from http://www.chicagojournal.com/main.asp?SectionID=48&SubSectionID=141&ArticleID=6466&TM=82880.45

Quadagno, J. (1994). *The color of welfare: How racism undermined the war on poverty*. New York: Oxford University Press.

Quinn, T. (2007). "You make me erect!": Queer girls of color negotiating heteronormative leadership at an urban all-girls' public school. *Journal of Gay and Lesbian Issues in Education, 4*(3), 31–47.

Reid, D. K. & Knight, M. G. (2006). Disability justifies exclusion of minority students: A critical history grounded in disability studies. *Educational Researcher, 35*(6), 18–23.

Risley, F. (1991, May 12). Focus: Restrictive covenants; from grass to garages, a litany of "don'ts." *The New York Times*. Retrieved May 14, 2008, from http://query.nytimes.com/gst/fullpage.html?res=9D0CE3DF1238F931A25756C0A967958260

Roberts, D. (2003). *Child welfare and civil rights*. Northwestern School of Law. Retrieved June 10, 2008, from www.northwestern.edu/ipr/people/robertsvita.pdf

Roediger, D. (1991). *Wages of whiteness: Race and the making of the American working class*. London: Verso Press.

Rofes, E. (2005). *Status quo or status queer. A radical rethinking of sexuality & schooling*. New York: Rowman & Littlefield.

Rojas, P. (2007). Are the cops in our heads and hearts? In INCITE! Women of Color against Violence (Eds.), *The revolution will not be funded: Beyond the non-profit prison industrial complex* (pp. 187–214). Boston, MA: South End Press.

Rosenbaum, J. (2009). Patient teenagers? A comparison of the sexual behavior of virginity pledgers and matched nonpledgers. *Pediatrics, 123*(1), pp. e110-e120.

Rousmaniere, K. (1999). Where Haley stood: Margaret Haley, teachers' work and the problem of teacher identity. In K. Weiler & S. Middleton (Eds.), *Telling women's lives: Narrative inquiries in the history of women's education* (pp. 147–161). Buckingham, UK: Open University Press.

Russell, S. (2008, April 25). Remembering Lawrence King: An agenda for educators, schools, and scholars. *Teachers College Record*. Retrieved July 7, 2008, from http://www.tcrecord.org ID Number: 15236

Ryan, J. (2004). Brown, school choice, and the suburban veto. *The Virginia Law Review, 90*, 1635–1647. Retrieved May 20, 2008, from http://64.233. 167.104/search?q=cache:oXNyGnsMezoJ:www.virginialawreview.org /content/pdfs/90/1635.pdf+segregation+academies+tradition&hl= en&ct=clnk&cd=10&gl=us

Saewyc, E., Poon, C., Homma, Y. & Skay, C. (2008). Stigma management? The links between enacted stigma and teen pregnancy trends among gay, lesbian and bisexual students in British Columbia. *Canadian Journal of Human Sexuality, 17*(3), 123–131.

Save Senn. (2006, November 3). Presentation to the Board of Education. Retrieved December 3, 2006, from http://savesenn.org/

Saxon, W. (1995, May 20). Albertis S. Harrison Jr., 88, dies: Led Virginia as segregation fell. *The New York Times*. Retrieved May 20, 2008, from http://query.nytimes.com/gst/fullpage.html?res=990CE5D81E3EF936A 15752C0A963958260

Schindler, P. (2005, April 29–May 5). Pope's views against gays are long and varied. *Downtown Express, 17*(49). Retrieved June 9, 2008, from http://www.downtownexpress.com/de_103/talkingpoints.com

Sedgwick, E. (2003). *Touching feeling: Affect, pedagogy, performativity.* Durham, NC: Duke University Press.

Sennett, R. (2008). *The craftsman.* New Haven, CT: Yale University Press.

The Sentencing Project. (2007). *Felony disenfranchisement laws in the United States.* Retrieved July 10, 2008, from www.sentencingproject.org/ Admin/Documents/publications/fd_bs_fdlawsinus.pdf

Silliman, J. & Bhatacharjee, A. (Eds.), (2002). *Policing the national body: Race, gender, and criminalization.* Boston, MA: South End Press.

Smith, A. (2005). *Conquest: Sexual violence and American Indian genocide.* Boston, MA: South End Press.

Social Justice High School. (2008). *Social Justice High School-Pride Campus.* Retrieved December 11, 2008, from http://sj.lvlhs.org/apps/pages/ index.jsp?uREC_ID=54003&type=d

Spring, J. (1996). *The American school: 1642–1996*. New York: McGraw-Hill.

Stacey, J. (1999, December). Ethnography confronts the global village: A new home for a new century? *Journal of Contemporary Ethnography, 28* (6), 687–697.

Stoler, A. (1995). *Race and the education of desire*. Durham, NC: Duke University Press.

Strauss, B. (2009, January 10). Successful CORE event raises hopes of stopping closings. *Catalyst*. Retrieved January 26, 2009, from http://www.catalystchicago.org/RUSSO/index.php/entry/1490/Successful_CORE_Event_Raises_Hopes_Of_Stopping_Closings

Stryker, S. (2008). *Transgender history*. Berkeley, CA: Seal Press.

Swanson C. & Barlage J. (2006, December). Influence: A study of the factors shaping education policy. *Education Week*. Retrieved July 12, 2008, from http://www.edweek.org/media/influence_execsum.pdf

Sycamore, M. (2006). *Nobody passes: Rejecting the rules of gender and conformity*. Emeryville, CA: Seal Press.

Sycamore, M., with Ruiz, J. (2008). The violence of assimilation: An interview with Mattilda aka Matt Bernstein Sycamore. *Radical History Review, 100*, 237–247.

Tamir, E. & Wilson, S. M. (2005). Who should guard the gates? Evidentiary and professional warrants for claiming jurisdiction. *Journal of Teacher Education, 56*, 332–342.

Telljohann, S., Price, J., Poureslami, M. & Easton, A. (1995, January). Teaching about sexual orientation by secondary health teachers. *Journal of School Health, 65*(1), 18–22.

Thousands march for immigrant rights: Schools, businesses feel impact as students, workers walk out. (2008, May 1). *CNN*. Retrieved October 6, 2008, from http://www.cnn.com/2006/US/05/01/immigrant.day/index.html

Tozer, S., Violas, P. & Senese, G. (1998). *School and society: Historical and contemporary perspectives*. Boston, MA: McGraw-Hill.

Trebay, G. (2008, June 22). He's pregnant. You're speechless. *The New York Times*. Retrieved February 2, 2009, from http://www.nytimes.com/2008/06/22/fashion/22pregnant.html

Tucker, J. (2006, November 15). San Francisco school board votes to dump JROTC program. *San Francisco Chronicle*, B1, Wednesday. Retrieved July 8, 2008, from http://www.sfgate.com/cgi-bin/article.cgi?f=/c/a/2006/11/15/BAG2HMD46B1.DTL

Tugend, A. (2005, April 6). Public military academies put discipline in schools. *The New York Times*. Retrieved April 24, 2009, from http://www.nytimes.com/2005/04/06/education/06academies.html

Turnbull, L. (2005, June 3). Homeowners find records still hold blot of racism. *The Seattle Times*. Retrieved May 13, 2008, from http://seattle times.nwsource.com/html/localnews/2002297312_covenants03m.html

United parents vote against school drill. (1929, February 12). *The New York Times*. Retrieved September 15, 2008, from http://nytimes.com/

United States Census Bureau. (2007, May 17). *Minority population tops 100 million*. Retrieved April 25, 2009, from http://www.census.gov/Press-Release/www/releases/archives/population/010048.html

Van Maanen, J. (1988). *Tales of the field: On writing ethnography*. Chicago, IL: The University of Chicago Press.

Wallace-Adams, D. (1988, February). Fundamental considerations: The deep meaning of Native American schooling, 1880–1900. *Harvard Educational Review*, 58(1), 1–28.

Warner, M. (1999). *The trouble with normal*. New York: Free Press.

Weiss, M. (2008, Winter). Gay shame and SM pride: Performative politics of sexual activism. *Radical History Review*, 100, 87–102.

West, C. (1997). Audacious democrats. In S. Fraser & J. Freeman (Eds.), *Audacious democracy: Labor, intellectuals, and the social reconstruction of America* (pp. 262–270). Boston, MA: Mariner.

Wilgoren, J. (2005, August 21). Politicized scholars put evolution on the defensive. *The New York Times*. Retrieved February 15, 2009, from http://www.nytimes.com/2005/08/21/national/21evolve.html?_r=1& ei=5094&en=88f0b94e7eb26357&hp=&ex=1124596800&partner=homep age&pagewanted=all

Williams, J. & Baron, K. (2007, October 7). Military sees big decline in black enlistees: Iraq war cited in 58% decline since 2000. *The Boston Globe*. Retrieved October 2, 2008, from http://www.boston.com/news/nation/washington/articles/2007/10/07/military_sees_big_decline_in_black_enlistees/

Williams, P. (1991). *The alchemy of race and rights: Diary of a law professor*. Cambridge, MA: Harvard University Press.

Williams, P. (2002, June 17). Racial privacy. *The Nation*. Retrieved January 15, 2009, from http://www.thenation.com/doc/20020617/williams

Wilson, C. (1995, October 18). Celebration puts Disney in reality's realm. *USA Today*, A1.

Wily Filipino. (2003).What the military taught me. Retrieved December 3, 2007, from http://www.thewilyfilipino.com/blog/archives/2003_03.html

Winant, H. (2004). *The new politics of race: Globalism, difference, justice*. Minneapolis, MN: University of Minnesota Press.

Winfield, A. (2007). *Eugenics and education in America: Institutionalized racism and the implications of history, ideology, and memory.* New York: Peter Lang.

Wolch, J. (1990). *The shadow state: Government and voluntary sector in transition.* New York, NY: The Foundation Center.

Woolf, V. (1938). *Three guineas.* Retrieved April 24, 2009, from http://ebooks.adelaide.edu.au/w/woolf/virginia/w91tg/chapter2.html

Yale Law Journal. (1973, June). *Segregation academies and state action, 82*(7), 1436–1461.

Yoshino, K. (2006a). *Covering: The hidden assault on our civil rights.* New York: Random House.

Yoshino, K. (2006b, January 15). The pressure to cover. *The New York Times Magazine.* Retrieved April 30, 2007, from http://www.nytimes.com/2006/01/15/magazine/15gays.html?ei=5090&en=089f6480fcfeb0e0&ex=1294981200&partner=rssuserland&emc=rss&pagewanted=print

Zehr, M. (2006, May). A clear stand: Religious schools are being pressed to spell out their policies regarding gay students and the children of same-sex couples. *Education Week, 25*(37), 27–30.

Zucchino, D. (1999). *The myth of the welfare queen.* New York: Scribner.

INDEX

A

AAA. *See* American Anthropological Association

AACTE. *See* American Association of Colleges for Teacher Education

ABA. *See* American Bar Association

Academic Freedom Act, 92

accreditation, teacher

Accredit Love, Not Condemnation campaign, 42–47

    historical background of, 35

    NCATE and, 35–36, 39

    queer rights and, 38–39, 55

Accredit Love, Not Condemnation campaign

    at Evangelical College, 42–44

    Evangelical College's response to, 45–47

    reflections on, 96, 99, 100

Acker, Sandra, 63

activism

    errors made, 95–96

    need for, 10, 41, 100–101

    personal growth and, 102

    pleasures of, 105–8

    policy research as, 90–94

    suggestions for, 103–4

    teacher accreditation and, 39

    in teaching, 69, 87–90

    vs. tolerance, 54–55

Addams, Jane, 106–7

AERA. *See* American Educational Research Association

African Americans

    military education and, 15, 19, 25

    in private schools, 52–53

    redlining and, 48–49

    restrictive covenants and, 47–48, 49

    social justice and, 67, 72, 90

    special education programs and, 88, 91

ALA. *See* American Library Association

American Anthropological Association (AAA), 40

American Association of Colleges for Teacher Education (AACTE), 44

American Bar Association (ABA), 39

American Educational Research Association (AERA)

    public policies and, 40–41

    reflections on, 96

    social justice and, 30–34, 37

American Library Association (ALA), 39

American Psychological Association, 40

anti-gay sentiments

    civil rights and, 92

    in education, 38, 54

    at Evangelical College, 42–47

    politics and, 2–3

archiving

    activism and, 104

    in participatory research, 9–10, 12

Arellano, Elvira, 66–67

Augustana College, 83

Aurora University, 83

Ayers, Bill, 33

B

Baker, Ella, 106

Baker, Eva, 30, 33–34

Beauboeuf-Lafontant, T., 87–88

The Bell Curve, 23

Benedictine University

    report card scores, 83

    response, 85–86

Benedict XVI (Pope), 56

Bethune, Mary McLeod, 64–65

Blackburn College, 83

Bob Jones University, 52

boot camp, 21

Bousquet, Marc, 10

Bradley University, 83

Brantlinger, Ellen, 90

Brecht, Bertolt, 105

Briggs Measure, 3

Brown, Jerry (Mayor), 19

Brown, Keith, 29

Bush, George H. W. (President), 48

Bush, George W. (President), 36, 48, 52, 92

Byrd, Harry (Senator), 51

C

Cantu, Cassandra, 22
Cato Institute, 92
Caucus of Rank and File Educators
    (CORE), 88
Chicago
    Feel Tank, 96–97
    female activism in, 66–67
    Junior Reserve Officers Training
        Corps (JROTC) in, 19–23
    racial targeting/discrimination in,
        15, 49
Chicago Public Schools (CPS)
    military education and, 19–23
    Nicholas Senn High School and, 13–
        16
    resources and creativity in, 25–28
Chicago State University, 83
choice, private, 2, 4
Christianity
    anti-gay covenant and, 43–47
    discrimination and, 52–53, 55–57
Cisneros, Sandra, 49–50
civil rights
    misleading initiatives, 92–93
    privatization and, 51–54
    professionalism and, 71–73
    See also social justice
clarity, political, 87–90
Clinton, Bill, 5
Columbia College, 83
Community Covenant, at Evangelical
    College, 42–47
Concordia University, 83
CORE. See Caucus of Rank and File
    Educators
court actions
    erasure and reframing in, 92–93
    flaunting and, 72
    queer issues and, 2–3
    restrictive covenants and, 48
covenants, restrictive
    discrimination and, 47–48, 49
    at Evangelical College, 42–47
covering
    discrimination and, 73–74
    in teaching, 71–72
Critical Resistance, 102

D

Daley, Richard M. (Mayor), 19, 20
Dangerous Minds, 68
Davis, Angela, 70
Defense of Marriage Act, 92
DeGeneres, Ellen, 2
De Jesus, Wilfredo (Reverend), 27
Department of Defense (DOD)
    gender and sexual violence and, 21–
        22
    schools, 19, 20, 24
DePaul University Chicago, 83
Diagnostic Statistics Manual, 101
discipline
    in Christian private schools, 52
    in military schools, 20–22, 55
    racial targeting and, 16, 18–19
    rethinking, 25–28
Discovery Institute, 93
discrimination
    covering and, 73–74
    gender identity and, 7, 15
    military education and, 15, 20–21
    redlining, 48–49
    restrictive covenants, 47–48, 49
diversity
    LGBTQ in education and, 76–77,
        86
    NCATE Standards and, 30–33, 37,
        44–45
    P-Project scoring for, 81
    teacher accreditation and, 39
DOD. See Department of Defense
Dohrn, Bernardine, 9
Dole, Bob, 52
Dominican University, 83
Don't Ask, Don't Tell policy, 15, 20, 23,
        24
Douglas, Sarah Mapps, 64–65
Duncan, Arne, 26, 88

E

Eastern Illinois University, 81, 84
EdLiberation, 88
educational disability programs, 88–89
Education Next, 19
education programs, teacher
    political curriculum in, 87–90

P Project assessment, 75–79
presentation outlining P Project, 79–
    81
recommendations, 82–83
results of assessment, 81–82
Elmhurst College, 84
emotions
    production/usefulness of, 97–100
    reflections on, 95–97
Employment Non-Discrimination Act
    (ENDA), 7
Erikson Institute, 84
eugenics
    educational assessment and, 89
    military education and, 23–24
    women and, 66–67
Eureka College, 84
Evangelical College
    Accredit Love, Not Condemnation
        campaign, 42–44
    campaign responses, 44–46
    Jane Addams Hull-House Museum
        event, 46–47

F

Factory and Workshop Bill, 106
Fair Housing Act (FHA), 48
Federal Home Loan Bank Board, 48
feelings. See emotions
Feel Tank Chicago, 96–97
feminists
    activism of, 65–66, 69, 90–92
    sex wars and, 56
Feminists for Life, 92
FHA. See Fair Housing Act
flaunting
    court action for, 72
    for social change, 100–104
    words, 58
Ford, Henry, 65
Foucault, Michel, 105
Freedom Writers, 68
free speech
    discrimination and, 54–57
    flaunting words and, 58
Freire, Paulo, 45

G

gated communities, 49–51
Gates, Bill, 36
gay marriage
    Arnold Schwarzenegger and, 1
    court rulings on, 2
    normative appearances and, 6–8
    Schwarzenegger, Arnold and, 2
gender identity
    discrimination and, 7, 15
    NCATE Standards and, 30–34
    P Project recommendations, 82–83
    teacher accreditation and, 39
    in teacher education programs, 79,
        81
gendering
    in the nursing profession, 67–68
    in social work, 65–66
    in the teaching profession, 63–65,
        68–69
Ghraib, Abu, 22
Gladwell, Malcolm, 26
Goffman, E., 97–98
Gollnick, Donna, 33
Gordon, Jenay, 75
Governor's State University, 84
Greaves, Dr. William, 26
Greenfeld, Lawrence A., 91
Greenville College, 84

H

Haley, Margaret, 45
Halstead, Morgan, 78
Harper, Helen, 64
Hebrew Theological College, 84
Heritage Foundation, 92
Herrnstein, Richard, 23
heteronormativity
    in education, 3, 62–65
    enforced ignorance and, 94
    gay marriage and, 6–8
    social justice and, 73
Heterosexuals Organizing for a Moral
    Environment (HOME), 56
History of Sexuality, 105
homophobia
    in education, 31
    in the military, 20–21, 24, 104

social justice and, 7, 18, 95
Horton, Myles, 45
housing, and discrimination, 47–51
Howenstein, Drea, 46
human rights. *See* civil rights; social
    justice

I

Illinois Association of Colleges for
    Teacher Education (IACTE), 43,
    46–47
Illinois College, 84
Illinois Institute of Technology, 84
Illinois Safe Schools Alliance, 75
Illinois State University, 82, 84
Illinois Wesleyan University, 84
*Influence: A Study of the Factors Shaping
    Education Policy*, 36
Irvine, Jacqueline Jordan, 52
Irvine, Janice, 93

J

Jaggar, A., 97–98
Jane Addams Hull-House Museum
    event flyer, 42
    forum event, 46
John Paul II (Pope), 56
Judson University, 84
Junior Reserve Officers Training Corps
    (JROTC)
    in Chicago, 19–23
    elimination of, 26
    See also military education

K

Keller Graduate School of Management
    of DeVry University, 84
Kendall College, 84
Kennedy, John F., 48
Keyes, Alan, 52
Knox College, 84
Kumashiro, Kevin, 42
Kushner, Tony, 56

L

Lake Forest College, 84
La Raza Educators in Los Angeles, 88
last authentic dude (LAD), teacher

archetype, 68–69
Lewis University, 84
LGBTQ (lesbian, gay, bisexual,
    transgender and queer)
    Accredit Love, Not Condemnation
        campaign, 42–47
    conservative Christianity and, 55–
        57
    Defense of Marriage Act and, 92
    NCATE Standards and, 30–34
    in teacher education programs, 75–
        79, 86
    See also queer body
Linton, S., 99–100
Loewen, James, 50
Lorde, A., 99
Low, Setha, 50
Loyola University Chicago, 84

M

MacKenzie, Dr. James, 25
MacMurray College, 84
Matsuda, Mari, 56
Matthew's Passion, 56
McCain, John, 2
McKendree College, 84
military education
    in Chicago, 19–23
    discipline techniques in, 20–21
    at Nicholas Senn High School, 13–
        16
    at Northeastern Illinois University,
        22
    rooting out queers and, 23–25
    school choice and, 17–19
Millikin University, 84
misogyny
    military education and, 21, 24, 104
    social justice and, 18
Monmouth College, 84
Mormonism, and diversity issues, 57
Murray, Charles, 23

N

Nader, Laura, 73, 101
National Advisory Committee on
    Institutional Quality and Integrity
    (NACIQI), 37

National Association of Real Estate
Boards, 48
National Council for the Accreditation of
Teacher Education (NCATE)
history of, 35
letter regarding Standards revisions,
30–32
privatization of public policy, 36
Professional Standards revisions,
29–30, 37
response to activism, 32–34, 40–41
social justice and, 37–39
National Education Association, 25
National Fair Housing Alliance
(NFHA), 48–49
National-Louis University, 84
Native women, and sterilization, 67, 91
Naval Academy, 13–16
NCATE. *See* National Council for the
Accreditation of Teacher Education
neoliberalism
characteristics of, 6, 8, 72
military education and, 17–18
in universities, 10
New York Coalition of Radical
Educators (NYCORE), 88
New York Times, 25
NFHA. *See* National Fair Housing
Alliance
Nicholas Senn High School
history of, 13–14
letter regarding Naval Academy,
14–15
response to activism, 15–16
Nightingale, Florence, 67–68
Nixon, Richard, 48
No Child Left Behind Act, 92
North Central College, 84
North, Connie, 78
Northeastern Illinois University
military education at, 22
report card scores, 84
Northern Illinois University, 84
North Park College, 84
Northwestern University, 84
nursing, and gendering, 67–68
NYCORE. *See* New York Coalition of
Radical Educators

O
Ogletree, Renae, 26–27
Olivet Nazarene University, 84
Outliers, 26

P
participatory research
archiving and, 9
characteristics of, 8–9
passing, 72
PBS. *See* Public Broadcasting Service
Pew Hispanic Trust, 6
Pfeiffer, MIchelle, 68
Polakow, Valerie, 90
Policy on Legislative and National Issues,
39
policy research, as activism, 90–94
political clarity, for educators, 87–90
P Project. *See* Pre-professional
Preparation Project
Preckwinkle, Toni (Alderwoman), 16
Pre-professional Preparation Project (P
Project)
assessment presentation, 79–81
initial survey, 75–79
recommendations, 82–83
results of assessment, 81–82
Pride Campus
formation of, 26–27
issues regarding, 27–28
Principia College, 84
private choice
in education, 2, 4
sexuality and, 70
private issues, vs. public issues, 5–8,
105–7
private schools
discrimination and, 52–53
teacher education programs and,
81–82
privatization
military education and, 17–18
NCATE and, 35–36, 41
public schools and, 58–59
resistance to, 100–101
privatopias, 49–50, 101
professionalism
as covering, 70–74

definition of, 69–70
white women and, 65–69
Proposition 54, 91
Public Broadcasting Service (PBS), 67
public education
    antievolution taught in, 92
    artists and queers in, 25–28
    bad, 14–15
    capitalism in, 10
    in Chicago. *See* Chicago Public
        Schools
    conservative Christianity and, 56–
        57
    heteronormativity in, 3
    military. *See* military education
    privatization and, 58–59
    school choice and, 17–19
    segregation in, 51–54
    the shadow state and, 36–38, 41
    social rights issues, 2, 9–10
    teacher education programs and,
        81–82
public policy
    vs. private issues, 5–8, 105–7
    privatizing of, 35–41

Q
queer body
    Bob Jones University and, 52–53
    covering and, 73–74
    in education, 3, 25–28
    power of, 1–2, 3
    public feelings and, 97–98
    rooting out of, 23–25
    teacher accreditation and, 38
    term usage, 1
    See also LGBTQ
Quincy University, 84

R
Racial Privacy Initiative, 91
racial targeting, 15, 18–19
    See also civil rights; discrimination;
        social justice
Rafferty, Max, 38
Reagan, Ronald, 48, 52, 91
Reconstruction era, 47–48
RED Campaign, 29, 33

redlining, 48–49
Rehnquist, William, 48
research
    participatory, 8–12
    policy, 90–94
Reserve Officers Training Corps
        (ROTC), 25
restrictive covenants
    discrimination and, 47–48, 49
    at Evangelical College, 42–47
Rethinking Schools (magazine), 85, 88
Rickover Naval Academy, 15–16
    See also military education
Roberts, Dorothy, 90
Roberts, John (Chief Justice), 92–93
Robinson, Sharon, 44
Rockford College, 85
Roosevelt University, 85
ROTC. *See* Reserve Officers Training
        Corps

S
Saint Xavier University, 85
San Francisco Board of Education, 26
School of the Art Institute of Chicago, 85
schools. *See* private schools; public
        education
Schwarzenegger, Arnold, 1, 2
Sedgwick, E., 94
segregation
    redlining and, 48–49
    restrictive covenants and, 47–48, 49
    in schools, 51–54, 88–89
sexual orientation
    NCATE Standards and, 30–34
    P Project recommendations, 82–83
    teacher accreditation and, 39
    in teacher education programs, 79,
        81
sexual violence, in the military, 21–22
shadow state, 36–38, 41
shame
    Evangelical College and, 41, 44, 45
    resistance to, 97–99
Shepard, Matthew, 56
Smith, Mary Ann, 13
social justice
    heteronormativity and, 73

NCATE and, 29–34, 36–38
organizations acting for, 39–40
policy research for, 90–94
public education and, 2, 9–10
suggestions for, 103–4
See also civil rights
social work, and gendering, 65–66
Solidarity Campus. *See* Pride Campus
Solomon, Alisa, 18
Southern Illinois University-Carbondale,
  82, 85
Southern Illinois University-
  Edwardsville, 82, 85
special education programs, 88–89
sterilization
  eugenics and, 24, 67
  of Native women, 67, 91
stigma, 98
Swank, Hilary, 68
Sycamore, Mattilda Bernstein, 2, 6, 11

T

TAME. *See* Teachers Against
  Militarized Education
Tate, William, 33–34
teacher accreditation
  Accredit Love, Not Condemnation
    campaign, 42–47
  historical background of, 35
  NCATE and, 35–36, 39
  queer rights and, 38–39, 55
  teacher education programs
  political curriculum in, 87–90
  P Project assessment, 75–79
  presentation outlining P Project, 79–
    81
  recommendations, 82–83
  results of assessment, 81–82
Teachers 4 Justice in San Francisco, 88
Teachers Against Militarized Education
  (TAME)
  campaign errors, 95
  history of, 25
  logo, 13
  See also military education
Teachers for Social Justice in Chicago, 88
teaching profession
  activism in, 69

gendering of, 63–65, 68–69
as politically relevant, 87–90
professionalism in, 70–74
special education programs, 88–89
stigma and shame within, 95–96
Till, Mamie, 101
tolerance
  vs. activism, 54–55
  problems with, 86–90
Transnational Association of Christian
  Colleges and Schools, 52
Triantafillou, Eric, 13
Trinity Christian College, 85
Trinity International University, 85

U

University of Chicago, 85
University of Illinois at Chicago, 82, 85
University of Illinois at Springfield, 82,
  85
University of Illinois at Urbana-
  Champaign, 82, 85
University of Mississippi, 52
University of Saint Francis, 85
U.S. Patriot Act, 92

V

Vanderbrook College of Music, 85
Village Voice, 18
Visibility Matters report cards
  grades, 83–85
  methods and grading scheme for,
    79–81
  recommendations, 82–83
  results, 81–82

W

Washington, Booker T., 5
website(s)
  AERA's, 33
  Illinois teacher education program,
    75–79
  NCATE's, 40
Western Illinois University, 81–82, 85
Wheaton College, 85
white lady bountiful (WLB), teacher
  archetype, 64–65, 68–69
whiteness

in nursing, 67–69
in social work, 65–66
in teaching, 63–65, 68–69
white supremacy
activism against, 90, 95
in education, 63, 65, 69
military education and, 24
privatization and, 51–52
Windy City Times (newspaper), 85
Wise, Arthur, 30, 37, 40
WLB. *See* white lady bountiful
women
activist work of, 66, 106–8
sexual abuse, in the military, 21–23
social injustices and, 67
teaching profession and, 64–65

Y

Yoshino, K., 71–72, 73